# THE
# TIBETAN
## WAY OF LIFE,
## DEATH AND REBIRTH

# THE
# TIBETAN
## WAY OF LIFE,
## DEATH AND REBIRTH

JOHN PEACOCK

DUNCAN BAIRD PUBLISHERS
LONDON

**The Tibetan Way of Life, Death and Rebirth**
John Peacock

First published in the United Kingdom and Ireland in 2003
by Duncan Baird Publishers Ltd
6th Floor, Castle House
75–76 Wells Street
London W1T 3QH

Conceived, created and designed by Duncan Baird Publishers

Project Editor: Peter Bently
Project Designer: Rebecca Johns
Picture Editor: Cecilia Weston-Baker
Commissioned Artwork: Sally Taylor (artistpartners ltd)

Managing Editor: Christopher Westhorp
Managing Designer: Dan Sturges

ISBN: 1-84483-057-8

10 9 8 7 6 5 4 3 2 1

Typeset in Sabon and Charlemagne
Colour reproduction by Scanhouse
Printed and bound in Singapore by Imago

NOTES
The abbreviations CE and BCE are used throughout this book:
CE  Common Era (the equivalent of AD)
BCE  Before the Common Era (the equivalent of BC)

Uncaptioned pictures are described on pages 143–144.

DEDICATION

This work is dedicated to my good
friend and colleague Paul Williams
for all his support over the years.

# CONTENTS

## GESHE THUPTEN JINPA, Ph.D.

# FOREWORD

Reading through the pages of *The Tibetan Way of Life, Death and Rebirth* is like being led through a vast and complex terrain by an experienced guide. Drawing from the Tibetan sources and, more specifically, from the ever-growing body of academic scholarship, the author brings together in this book, in a wonderfully lucid and coherent presentation, the key elements of the Tibetan religious world.

Beginning with the pre-Buddhist Tibetan world view and myths, the author tells the fascinating story of the early history of Buddhism in Tibet, the struggles between the native Bön religion and the new faith, and the eventual emergence of what are today the four main schools of Tibetan Buddhism. The reader is also brought face to face with the rich belief systems of the Tibetan people, including the philosophical ideas that underpin the complex religious practices.

Through quotations from original texts and an amazing array of images, the author evokes for the reader the deep sense of awe the Tibetan people feel for their natural environment, their understanding of life, their fervent devotion to the vision of universal compassion as symbolized by the divine figure of the Buddha of compassion, their veneration of the Buddhist ideal of monastic life, and, finally, their deeply spiritual approach to the question of death. The reader is also shown glimpses of the profiles of some of the most important historical figures of Tibetan Buddhism, including the Dalai Lamas.

Often people have asked me what book they should read as a good introduction to Tibetan Buddhism, something both accessible and at the same time comprehensive. I have always found this question difficult to answer. Now I can reply, without hesitation, "Read John Peacock's beautiful book, *The Tibetan Way of Life, Death and Rebirth*".

*Thupten Jinpa*

Geshe Thupten Jinpa Ph.D.
*Montreal, Canada.*
*Principal English Translator to*
*His Holiness the Dalai Lama.*

# INTRODUCTION

Tibetan religion can appear at times to be a bewildering combination of both the rational and the magical. It embraces a plethora of distinct and diverse traditions, from the Buddhism of the great monasteries to the folk religion of the ordinary Tibetan. Moreover, the character of this religion has been shaped and moulded by the startling landscape of Tibet itself, which is known to Tibetans as "the Land of Snows" (P'ö). A vast high-altitude region the size of Western Europe, it is seen to those who live there as both a frightening and enchanting environment.

The landscape is dominated by the great mountains that encircle and divide it, and the sky under which humanity struggles to exist in the face of the immensity of nature, by turns benevolent and destructive. This environment, capable of both uplifting and crushing the human spirit, gave rise to the traditional Tibetan world view in which imagination is a dominant factor. In early pre-Buddhist culture, the inescapable and ever-present natural forces were personified as divine and demonic powers, and Tibet was transformed into a living and active landscape teeming with features that were accorded sacred significance. It is hardly surprising that pilgrimage to holy sites should become, for Tibetans, a major form of religious expression.

When Buddhism entered Tibet, its ideas were sown upon fertile ground. The adaptation of indigenous elements to the new religion was made easier because of the apparent similarities between local traditions and the ethos of what was to be the primary expression of Buddhism in Tibet, namely Tantra (Gyud), a form of practice whose origin is attributed to the Buddha. Many local deities of pre-Buddhist origin were co-opted as protectors of the Buddhist path and teachings. Indeed, Tibetan Buddhism is infused with indigenous pre-Buddhist beliefs, and it is this potent mixture, rather than the "orthodox" doctrines and philosophies of the great Buddhist monasteries, that governs the daily life of the ordinary people and finds expression in "folk religion". However, monastic Buddhism itself is a complex amalgam of esoteric

Indian Buddhist doctrines and practices mixed with indigenous elements, from which arose a number of schools and sects in the course of Buddhism's diffusion in Tibet.

Tantric Buddhism, or Vajrayana, is what distinguishes Tibetan Buddhism from the Buddhism found in countries such as Sri Lanka, Burma, Thailand, China and Japan (with the exception of one form of Japanese Buddhism). It is a development of a late Indian form of Mahayana Buddhism that appears to have originated in Bengal and the Swat Valley (in contemporary northern Pakistan). Its teachings are preserved in a voluminous literature translated from Sanskrit into Tibetan and containing 4,567 individual works attributed to the Buddha and to Indian *pandit*s (masters). In a huge number of cases the originals of these writings do not survive, owing to the demise of Buddhism in India, the land of its birth, in the Middle Ages: Tibetan Buddhism is therefore crucially important as virtually the sole repository of the wisdom of Indian Tantric Buddhism. However, there is an equally vast literature written by Tibetan teachers and masters (*lama*s) within the four main schools of Tibetan Buddhism, and the production of religious writings continues today.

*The Tibetan Way of Life, Death and Rebirth* is intended to be an introductory guide to the complex phenomenon of Tibetan religious and spiritual traditions. Tibetan Buddhism is naturally central to this guide, permeating as it does almost all aspects of Tibetan life both within Tibet itself and in the worldwide Tibetan diaspora caused by the Chinese occupation since the 1950s. Despite its great antiquity, Tibetan Buddhism offers psychological insights which, together with its emphasis on the development of wisdom and compassion, continue to speak to us today. Tibetans emphasize that one thing is absolutely certain (death) and one thing absolutely uncertain (its timing), and from this basic premise arises a belief system which, far from dwelling morbidly on death, strives above all to instruct us how to live in harmony both with ourselves and with one another.

# A LANDSCAPE OF THE SPIRIT

There are many legends and myths surrounding the creation of the land of Tibet, nearly all of them with roots in the indigenous pre-Buddhist religion of Bon and in folk culture. These accounts are usually structured around the bringing of order out of chaos, with order represented as good and chaos as evil. Creation myths also include the generation of a sacred geography, wherein the very landscape of Tibet is of sacred significance. Mountains in particular are greatly revered by Tibetans as the point of contact between heaven and earth.

# RADIANT AND
# BLACK MISERY

Tibetan legends testify to an inseparable sacred connection between the land of Tibet and its peoples that long predates the arrival of Buddhist ideas and practices. After the advent of Buddhism, the ancient "folk religion" (*mi cho*), with its emphasis on the powers of nature, continued to flourish and Buddhism sought to absorb it rather than eliminate it. Where this absorption was not entirely successful it is possible to observe all three strands of Tibetan belief – *mi cho*, Buddhism and Bon (see box on opposite page) – within religious practice.

The spiritual life of lay Tibetans will therefore encompass many practices and beliefs derived from Bon and the pre-Buddhist folk traditions, which are extremely ancient and show considerable regional variation. Most people will be familiar from childhood with a wealth of stories and songs derived from the folk tradition that recount epic deeds and magical happenings. For ordinary Tibetans the world teems with signs and meanings that present themselves continually and are subject to interpretation. These various unseen forces of existence are understood as inducing catastrophe or assisting with the difficulties of life, which is viewed as a continuous struggle to defend oneself and one's home against malign

A Tibetan monk of the Nyingma order near Guinan in Kham, now part of China's Qinghai province. Tibet's oldest school of Buddhism, the Nyingma incorporates many influences from pre-Buddhist traditions.

powers. At the same time, beneficent forces have to be invoked in order to bring wealth and prosperity to the family. While an over-reliance on such worldly forces is discouraged, outside the monastic community there is no prohibition on people performing often elaborate rituals to propitiate the gods and other unseen forces. For example, a traditional Tibetan dwelling incorporates "houses" or "seats" for the *pho lha* and *phuk lha*, respectively the male and female deities who are invoked in daily rituals to protect the household from malevolent forces.

A world view in which human beings are seen to be caught between malign and benign forces is reflected in a number of creation myths preserved within the folk

## THE WAY OF BON

Tibet's official religion before the arrival of Buddhism, Bon was primarily concerned with the maintenance of cosmic order and the relationship between humans and the gods. Its priests (*shen*) sought to ensure the fortunes of the state by means of complex rites involving sacrifice – including human sacrifice. To maintain the cosmic order, the *shen* recited complicated cosmogonies and genealogies, particularly at funerals.

With the advent of Buddhism, Bon was not suppressed nor did it disappear. It developed a closer relationship with the folk religion, and Bon elements can be observed to this day in the practices of ordinary Tibetans. Miwo Shenrap (eighth century CE) introduced many Buddhist elements into Bon, but the influence was not all one way, as seen by the adoption of many Bon deities as "Dharma protectors" (see pages 74–77).

tradition. They are very ancient in origin and may have some connection with earlier Indian and Iranian beliefs. These colourful accounts show us the creation of a universe in which the forces of good and evil co-exist.

One myth speaks of a primary god of the universe, Yangdak Gyalpo, who existed before the sun, moon, seasons and time came into being. This is a god of pure potentiality, out of which are born a white light and a black light, which in turn give birth to two male beings. A white being emerges out of the white light and a black being from the black light. The black being is said to represent pure negation and is called Black Misery (Myalwa Nakpo). From this being emerge the constellations, the

## THE GODDESS AND THE MONKEY

According to a Tibetan Buddhist legend, when the world was first created there were no human beings. The *bodhisattva* of compassion, Avalokiteshvara, and his consort, Tara, sent their incarnations into Tibet. Avalokiteshvara's incarnation took the form of a macaque monkey while Tara's was a cannibal ogress called Tagsen Mo. The monkey took strict vows of celibacy and lived in meditative seclusion, but Tagsen Mo was very lonely and cried and sang about her loneliness.

The monkey heard the desperate cries of the ogress and was filled with compassion. Tagsen Mo urged him to marry her, but he initially refused because of his vows. However, he agreed after consulting Avalokiteshvara and the couple produced six children, said to be the progenitors of the six classes of being that inhabit the universe: gods, demigods, humans, hungry ghosts, animals and denizens of hell. The six offspring in turn produced the first Tibetans.

demons, drought, disease and all kinds of misery. It is at this point that the demonic forces are said to begin their sinister work in the world. In contrast, the white being is termed Radiant (O' Zerden) and is seen as the principle behind all that is good in the world. Contemporary scholarship shows a clear link between this myth and some early forms of Iranian belief known as Zurvanism, an antecedent of Manicheanism, a doctrine which taught that everything springs from two sources: light (good) and darkness (evil).

Such dualism is present in other Tibetan accounts in which the figure of a creator appears. This creator manifests the universe from pure potentiality. One such myth recounts how, out of the breath of the creator, there emerged the syllables *hu hu*, which in turn gave rise to two beings: Good Father (Phen Yap), who came out of a white egg, and Evil Father (Nod Yap), who sprang from a black egg. The beneficent Good Father is described as the Lord of Being (Yoe Pa) and is the source of all goodness, while Evil Father is the Lord of Non-Being (Med Pa) and is the source of all the evil in the world. These two beings create the entire manifest universe. The beneficent god is the progenitor of eighteen brothers and sisters, nine male and nine female, whose own progeny are all the divine beings. The malevolent god is said to create evils such as demons, plague, famine, illness, violence and suffering in general. To him are credited all the forces of negativity and destruction.

One more Tibetan creation myth is worth recounting because it happens, coincidentally, to be supported by modern science. According to one tradition, it is said that Tibet once lay beneath the sea but eventually rose to become the highest country in the world. Intriguingly, this is something that has actually been confirmed: the vast Tibetan plateau, and the Himalayan mountains which border it to the south, were created millions of years ago by the collision of the Indian subcontinent – then an island – with the massive landmass to its north. Much of this landmass was once under water, as demonstrated by the remains of amphibious dinosaurs (ichthyosaurs) discovered on the southern edge of the Tibetan plateau – which continues to rise at the rate of about 1–2cm (0.4–0.8 inches) a year.

# THE CELESTIAL KINGS

Early Tibetan history is shrouded in mystery. However, many myths and legends have been passed down from generation to generation, and these stories constitute a "mythological history" for Tibetans. The accounts are generally in the service of teachings about the spread of Buddhism in Tibet.

Tibetan history, in the way that people in the West would commonly understand it, really begins in the seventh century CE with the coming of Buddhism in the reign of Srongtsen Gampo (see page 20). However, he is traditionally said to have been preceded by thirty kings, commencing with Tibet's first seven mythological rulers, who occupied the "seven heavenly thrones".

The legends claim that the first king of Tibet was called Nyatri Tsanpo, "He who was carried on the back to victory". Little or nothing is known about this figure, who would almost certainly have been a practitioner of the Bon religion (see box on page 13). However, one legend claims that Nyatri Tsanpo was descended from the Shakya royal family, the north Indian dynasty which four or five hundred years earlier had produced the Buddha, who is known as Shakyamuni, "the

The hero of a huge body of Tibeto-Mongolian myth, Gesar Ling (left) agreed to descend from heaven to fight demons only if granted a flying horse, magical weaponry and heroic companions. Mongolia has close cultural connections with Tibet and is the origin of this painting.

Sage of the Shakyas". It is also claimed that Nyatri Tsanpo and the six kings who ruled after him were not mortals but descended from heaven to earth by a sacred thread that connected the two realms. These kings were said to return to heaven by the same route, vanishing "like the rainbow". The kings of Tibet became mortal only after the thread that connected heaven and earth was severed by King Gri Gum (see box below).

Another significant legendary king is Gesar Ling, whose life and exploits are preserved in numerous popular songs and poems. The material preserving these legends is some of the oldest in Tibetan and dates back as far as the seventh century CE. Gesar

## THE THREAD OF HEAVEN

The eighth king of Tibet was Gri Gum, which means "killed by the knife". He appears to be a heretic within the Bon tradition in a similar way to that in which King Lang Darma is viewed within Tibetan Buddhism (see page 22): both are said to oppose the prevailing religion. Like his predecessors, Gri Gum descended from heaven via a cord that bound heaven to earth. However, Gri Gum had an argument with one of his ministers and fell under a magical spell that caused him to sever the cord. This act rendered him mortal and he had to find an alternative way of gaining heaven. Thus upon his assassination – like Lang Darma, Gri Gum was said to

have been killed by one of his ministers to put an end to his religious persecutions – Gri Gum's corpse was placed in a coffin and thrown into a river.

The cycle of legends surrounding Gri Gum probably represents a stage in the development of Bon which stressed earthly deities in opposition to heavenly ones. Following Gri Gum's death, there was a significant shift in the way that funerary rites were carried out and a form of Bon developed known as Dur Bon ("Bon of Funerary Rites") which placed greater emphasis on the return of the body to the earth. From this time, great importance was accorded to the construction of royal tombs.

is also known as Pu Gye ("Hairy Prince") and is considered to be of divine origin. He is noteworthy in being a warrior king, and many of the stories about him tell of wars waged with China. Prior to the advent of Buddhism, the Tibetans were considered to be a warlike people – it was only with the aid of Tibetan troops that the Tang emperor of China succeeded in crushing a serious rebellion in 763CE.

It is with the figure of King Lhatho Thori that we perceive the first tentative connection with Buddhism. Like many of the kings before him, Lhatho Thori was a warrior. In his seventy-ninth year, while on the roof of his palace of Yambu Lhakhang, he watched in wonder as a chest descended in a ray of light. Upon opening it the king discovered a number of Buddhist religious works (*sutra*s) and the six-syllable *mantra Om mani padme hum* that was to assume such importance in Tibet (see page 101).

Neither Lhatho Thori nor any of his ministers could read what was written in these books. In a dream, the Buddha appeared to the king and informed him that the meaning of these works would not be known for five generations, when a stranger would come to Tibet and unlock their secrets. Despite the inaccessibility of the *sutra*s, they were honoured as being of profound significance, and through his veneration of them Lhatho Thori became a young man again and lived to be 120. He was later revered as an emanation of the *bodhisattva* Samantabhadra, who is considered to be the symbol of universal benevolence and goodness.

Mythical history as recounted in the Tibetan chronicles points to a world that is both dramatic and infused with distress and ecstasy. Such history depends not on the usual sense of historical continuity as we would understand it in the West but on the merging of the human psyche with landscape and the realm of the senses. Tibetan mythology sees human activity as indissolubly linked with the mythic world, and the intuitive insights furnished by this link are employed to provide protection from the vagaries of sickness, death, ill fortune, pain and distress. In traditional Tibet, mythical knowledge is thus both a source of sustenance and also the foundation for the Tibetans' sense of their place in the world – and the means by which they can explore that world and access their own potentiality for being.

# SHAMBALA AND SHANGRI-LA

Human beings have always hankered after a perfect world and religious traditions around the world testify to this in an endless proliferation of myths about "golden eras" and heavenly abodes. In the twentieth century, Tibet itself came to occupy just such a position in the Western imagination as the location of Shangri-La, the mythical paradise in James Hilton's novel *Lost Horizon*.

Hilton's Shangri-La appears to be based on the genuine ancient Tibetan myth of Shambala. Said to lie to the north of Tibet, it is a kingdom surrounded by high snowy peaks with, at its centre, a huge city dominated by the king's palace. The kings of

Shambala are also priests, who are said to have received teaching directly from the Buddha. It is in Shambala that a final battle will take place between the forces of good and evil, religion and atheism.

It is believed that the current age is one in which the Dharma, the Buddha's teaching, is in decline. Things will deteriorate further until one day lawlessness, violence and hatred dominate and even infect the land of Shambala, except only the great city itself. When the vice and corruption of the world finally reach the city walls, the king of Shambala will muster his armies of gods and ride forth from his palace to destroy the forces of evil.

# SUBDUING THE DEMONS

According to Tibetan chronicles, Buddhism arrived in Tibet in the seventh century during the reign of the historical King Srongtsen Gampo (569–650CE). In reality the first Buddhist teachers from India and Central Asia probably entered Tibet considerably before this. Nevertheless, it is to Srongtsen Gampo that the establishment of Buddhism is traditionally attributed, and he came to be revered as an incarnation of Avalokiteshvara, the *bodhisattva* of compassion.

Srongtsen Gampo was the fifth king in line of succession from Lhatho Thori (see page 18) and initially, like his predecessors, he was a practitioner of Bon. It is traditionally held that Srongtsen Gampo adopted Buddhism under the influence of his two devoutly Buddhist queens, Wengchen and Bhrikuti Devi, who were from China and Nepal respectively. The two consorts brought sacred images and founded temples and are revered as incarnations of the *bodhisattva* Tara – Wengchen of White Tara and Bhrikuti of Green Tara (see pages 70–71).

It is said that Buddhist texts were first translated into Tibetan in the reign of Srongtsen Gampo, who invited many translators from

This magnificent gilt and jewel-encrusted statue of the Buddha is known as the Jowo Rinpoche. Tradition has it that it was brought to Tibet by Wengchen, Srongtsen Gampo's Chinese queen.

Kashmir and India to Lhasa, the Tibetan capital. The king also sent the scholar Thomi Sambhota to India to develop an alphabet for the Tibetan language, which until then had had no written form. With the aid of Indian scholars, Thomi Sambhota devised an alphabet – a syllabary would be more accurate – modelled on a Sanskrit script. He is also said to have written the first systematic grammar of the Tibetan language.

Despite the orthodox tradition, the early chronicles do not offer any real proof of Srongtsen Gampo's conversion to Buddhism, or even of his active support for it. It is only in the eighth century CE, during the reign of Trisong Detsen (756–797CE), that there is clear state sponsorship of Buddhism, which eventually culminates in the

## THE HEART OF THE DEMON

Tibet's holiest temple is probably one of its oldest, the Tsulhakhang ("House of Wisdom") in Lhasa. Also known as the Jokhang ("House of the Lord [Buddha]"), it is home to the Jowo Rinpoche, a statue of the Buddha that is Tibet's most revered sacred image (see illustration, opposite).

The Jokhang was built in the seventh century by King Srongtsen Gampo to mark the arrival of his Nepalese queen, Bhrikuti Devi, and has been added to over the centuries. As with many temples in Tibet, there is a myth associated with the founding of the Jokhang that represents the triumph of Buddhism over the indigenous Bon deities. The Tibetan chronicles recount how the temple was built on the site of a lake in Lhasa that was identified as the heart of a great female demon, and in which visions of the

future could be seen. Before the Jokhang could be built the lake was filled in and the demon, who represented the power of the old religion, was exorcised.

foundation of Tibet's first Buddhist monastery at Samye. Tradition has it that Trisong Detsen invited two of Tibetan Buddhism's most revered founder-figures, Shantarakshita and Padmasambhava, to come from India to teach the Dharma. According to legend, Shantarakshita's teaching so angered the Bon deities who controlled Tibet that they visited a host of catastrophes – famine, floods and earthquakes – on the land. Forced to return home, Shantarakshita prophesied the arrival of Padmasambhava, a teacher with the skill and power to subdue Tibet's hostile demons.

More historically, the Bon hierarchy saw the arrival of Buddhism increasingly as a threat to their power and privileges and sought to limit its influence if not eradicate it

## LANG DARMA THE APOSTATE

The closest Buddhism ever came to being eradicated in Tibet was in the reign of King Lang Darma (836–842CE), who is said to have been driven by demons to restore the Bon religion. Lang Darma's persecution of Buddhism saw monasteries destroyed, libraries burned and many monks slain. The king's violent campaign can in part be explained by real political and economic motives. There was growing disenchantment with the power and arrogance of the monasteries, which were free from taxation and supported by a sizeable proportion of the population, who were diverted into agricultural labour.

After six years on the throne, Lang Darma was murdered by a Buddhist monk at a performance of the Black Hat dance (see illustration opposite page). Performances of the dance to this day commemorate the murder, which Tibetan Buddhists view as a compassionate act by the monk aimed at preventing Lang Darma from accumulating further negative *karma*.

As a result of Lang Darma's persecution, the practice of Buddhism in Tibet degenerated into little more than superstition and magic. It took many years to re-establish contact with the Buddhist communities of India and China, both of which had been the motivating forces behind the dissemination of Buddhism in Tibet. However, the resurgence of Bon proved, ultimately, to be relatively short-lived.

A dancer taking part in the Shanak, or Black Hat dance, at Rumtek monastery in Sikkim, a culturally Tibetan region of India between Nepal and Bhutan. The dance commemorates the assassination in 842CE of King Lang Darma, whom Tibetan tradition regards as a great persecutor of Buddhism.

entirely. The dispute between the pro-Buddhist and Bon factions led to violent clashes, with the result that Shantarakshita was obliged to leave the country, returning only many years later.

Padmasambhava is said to have originated in Uddiyana, an area that roughly corresponds to the Swat valley in modern Pakistan. He too was summoned to Tibet by Trisong Detsen, but as he approached the frontier the hostile Bon gods are said to have unleashed thunderbolts, hail, wind and driving snow to deter him from entering the country, before blocking a canyon to bar his progress. In response Padmasambhava simply seated himself in meditation, and by the power of his meditative experience he converted the demons into Dharmapalas, "protectors of the Dharma" (see pages 74–77). He went on to subdue and convert hostile and demonic forces across the length and breadth of Tibet.

Some Tibetan sources claim that Padmasambhava remained in Tibet until the consecration of the monastery at Samye, performing an exorcism of demons before work on the monastery could begin in earnest. In other accounts he left Tibet immediately after subduing the country's demons; if so, the building of Samye would probably have been overseen by Shantarakshita, who by this time had returned to Tibet. Modelled on the Indian monastery of Otantapuri, Samye was completed in 779CE.

# THE HEART OF HEAVEN

This anonymous Tibetan poem dates from the ninth century CE. As well as telling of the mythological origins of the kings of Tibet, who are said to have descended from heaven to earth (see pages 16–17), the poem is a eulogy to the outstanding natural beauty of the Tibetan landscape. It begins with an account of the first king, Nyatri Tsanpo, descending from the heavens onto a sacred mountain.

"Descended from the six Lords, the gods
   of the ancestors,
Who dwell above mid-heaven,
He descended from the heights of the
   heavens....

He came as the sovereign protector on
   the face of the earth,
He came as rain which covers the face
   of the earth.
When he came to the holy mountain
   of Gyang-do,
The great mountain bowed low in
   reverence, bowed low in reverence.
The blue water of the springs rippled and
   the trees came together in homage,
And even the very rocks honoured him.
The passing cranes also gave salutation.
As Lord of the six regions of Tibet he came,
And when he first came to this world,
As the Lord of all under heaven he entered
   the world.

This is the heart of heaven,
This is the centre of the world.
Ringed by snowy peaks,
The origin of all rivers,
Where the mountains are towering and
   the land is pure.
Country so excellent,
Where men are born as sages and heroes,
And follow good laws.
This country is a land of swift horses,
And he chose it for its unexcelled qualities.
The King, whose religion is equalled by
   none,
Is worshipped even by the cranes and takes
   the very light as his wrap!"

# THE BELL
# AND THE
# THUNDERBOLT

When Buddhism came to Tibet it brought with it the full panoply of Indian religious ideas, including the doctrines of *karma* and rebirth. Differing approaches to these teachings find expression in the various schools and sects of Tibetan Buddhism, each of which has its own distinctive outlook on how to pursue the supreme Buddhist goal of awakening, or enlightenment. Crucial to this pursuit is the guidance of a wise and learned teacher (*lama*), and Tibetans honour many such masters – some of whom are revered as manifestations of divine beings.

# THE GREAT VEHICLE

Tradition holds that the Buddha was born near Lumbini in what is now Nepal and raised in the royal palace of his father, the ruler of the Shakya clan. He was born Siddhartha Gautama and only later came to be called "Buddha", a Sanskrit word for someone who has attained the extraordinary feat of "enlightenment" or, more accurately, "awakening" (*bodhi*). The Buddha is said to have "awoken" to the nature of reality – the way things really are. The dates of his long life are much debated, but it seems likely that he died aged eighty toward the end of the fifth century BCE.

It is said that Siddhartha's father confined his son to the palace in order to screen him from the realities of life, namely old age, sickness and death. But Siddhartha's

curiosity was too great, and on secret excursions from the palace he came face to face with these realities. He also encountered a wandering mendicant or ascetic, who had renounced all worldly ties to seek spiritual truth.

These encounters led Siddhartha to leave the palace in search of a means to overcome the *duhkha* (pain, distress, suffering and "unsatisfactoriness") associated with the human condition. For many years he practised the severe austerities of the *yogin* in the forests of

Tibetan nuns meditating next to the Mahabodhi temple at Bodh Gaya, Bihar, India. The temple was erected in the 6th century CE next to the Bodhi Tree ("Tree of Awakening"), said to be a descendant of the very one under which the Buddha attained awakening. Legend tells how the Buddha's path to awakening encompassed many hundreds of births, of which his birth as Siddhartha Gautama was the last.

northeast India, but failed to attain awakening. This led to the first of his insights: he saw that the spiritual quest is impossible if one is either distracted by excessive materialism or tormented by excessive physical want. Buddhism is often described as a "Middle Way" between these extremes.

Abandoning his life of asceticism, Siddhartha resolved to engage in meditation as a means to further his spiritual search. At what is now Bodh Gaya in northeastern India, he sat beneath a species of fig tree (*Ficus religiosa*). On the night of the full moon in May, after having been assailed in vain by Mara (a demonic figure symbolizing evil thoughts and desire), Siddhartha attained awakening. The Buddha had discovered

# THE NOBLE TRUTHS AND THE EIGHTFOLD PATH

Succinctly formulated, the "Four Noble Truths" are the Buddha's expression of the problem of existence and the way to overcome it: 1. *Duhkha* (pain, distress, suffering, anxiety and "unsatisfactoriness") exists. 2. The cause of *duhkha* is *trishna* (craving, desire). 3. There is a means to end *duhkha*. 4. The means to end *duhkha* is the Noble Eightfold Path.

It has been suggested that the form of the Four Noble Truths is based on early Indian medical diagnostic practice. To the Buddha, our malady is *duhkha* – we experience life as unsatisfactory or painful. He goes on to identify *trishna* ("craving", literally "unquenchable thirst"). He insists that there is a "cure" for *duhkha* and identifies this as the Noble Eightfold Path.

This path is composed of "right view, right thought, right speech, right action, right livelihood, right effort, right mindfulness and right concentration". These are subdivided into three groups: insight or understanding (*prajnya* – right view and right thought); morality (*shila* – right speech, right action and right livelihood) and meditation (*samadhi* – right effort, right mindfulness and right concentration).

In Tibet, manuscripts of Buddhist teachings are usually broad rectangles (a format derived from early Buddhist scriptures, which were written on palm leaves) and enclosed between wooden covers. This 13th-century cover is painted on the inside with a central panel showing the goddess Prajnyaparamita (the embodiment of wisdom) flanked by *bodhisattva*s. The smaller panels show other deities and *lama*s.

what he later expressed in his first teaching as the "Four Noble Truths" (see box on page 29). The Buddha's state of awakening is also referred to in Sanskrit as *nirvana*. This is often understood in the West as some sort of heaven or "thing" that the Buddha attained, but in fact the word is not a noun but a verb, literally "*nirvana*-ing". This means that the Buddha continued to act in the world – he taught for forty-five years afterwards – but with a consciousness transformed from that which sustains *samsara*. This is another Sanskrit term, meaning the cycle of birth, death and rebirth, together with its attendant *duhkha*. Only outside *samsara* is freedom from *duhkha* said to lie.

Of vital importance to the process of mental transformation is the practice of meditation (*bhavana*), more accurately the "cultivation" of wholesome states of mind. The two most important forms are "calming meditation" (*shamatha bhavana*) and "insight meditation" (*vipashyana bhavana*). In the first, one seeks to calm the mind through techniques generally involving some form of concentration. Having achieved this, one attempts to access "insight" into the truths of "impermanence" and "not-self" (see pages 32–33). All meditation emphasizes the cultivation of awareness. Another practice is "meditation on loving kindness" (*maitri*), one of the central Buddhist virtues that is seen as a prerequisite for the development of compassion (*karuna*).

The Buddhism of Tibet is derived from a form that flowered in India in the early centuries CE. Known as the Mahayana ("Great Vehicle"), it claimed to have a different vision of the goal of Buddhism from other forms that Mahayanists referred to pejoratively as Hinayana ("Lesser Vehicle"). The central figure in the Mahayana vision was the *bodhisattva* ("Buddha-to-be"), a being so motivated by compassion (*karuna*) for all suffering that he or she committed to the "*bodhisattva* path" – the long, arduous road to buddhahood (see pages 64–67). Anyone aspiring to follow the *bodhisattva* path must cultivate the "perfections" (see box below). But before this, it is necessary to develop the "awakening-mind" or *bodhichitta*. According to the great Indian teacher Shantideva, *bodhichitta* took two forms, "the mind resolved on awakening" (that is, one who wishes to embark on the path) and the "mind proceeding toward awakening" (one who is actually on the path, motivated by altruism toward all beings).

## THE PERFECTIONS

At the very heart of the practice of the Mahayana vision of Buddhism are the development of the "perfections" (*paramitas*), or virtues, which are deemed absolutely essential to anyone embarking on the path of the *bodhisattva*. These perfections are: generosity (*dana*), morality (*shila*), patience (*kshanti*), vigour (*virya*), advanced meditation (*dhyana*) and understanding (*prajnya*). Sometimes this list is extended to include a further four perfections – "skill in means" (*upaya*), conviction (*pranidhana*), strength (*bala*) and knowledge (*jnana*). The *paramitas*, in the words of one famous Buddhist text (the *Lankavatara Sutra*), are "ideals of spiritual perfection, designed to act as guidance on the *bodhisattva*'s path to self-realization ... they are to be seen as ideals for worldly life (*dana* and *shila*), then as ideals for the emotional life (*shanti* and *virya*), and finally as ideals for the spiritual life (*dhyana* and *prajnya*)".

Another feature of Mahayana Buddhism is its unique doctrine of "emptiness" (*shunyata*). This teaching can be seen as an extension of the teaching of "not-self" (*anatman*) found in early Buddhism. Emptiness specifically means the denial of "intrinsic existence" within all phenomena. If something possessed intrinsic existence, it is argued, it would exist independently of anything else. However, the Buddha claimed that all things are "dependently originated" – everything arises from, and depends on, something else – and hence are "empty" of intrinsic existence. What we call a table, for example, is only a "mind-projected" form. The deluded mind manifests an independent existence for the table which in reality it does not possess.

## WORDS OF THE DHARMA

Tibetan Buddhism has one of the largest literatures of any Buddhist culture. After the creation of a Tibetan script (see page 21), there was a prodigious period of translation, generally called the "First Diffusion", in Tibet. Many writings (*sutras* and *tantras*) were translated, mostly from ancient Indian Sanskrit. This

activity was ended by King Lang Darma in the ninth century CE (see page 22). By the tenth century, a "Second Diffusion" had begun under the patronage of the ngari rulers of western Tibet – a period that witnessed the work of the great Rinchen Zangpo. Many *sutras* and *tantras* were translated as well as works about logic, rhetoric, astrology and metaphysics.

In the fourteenth century, the great scholar Puton Rinpoche edited the mass of religious literature to produce the *Kanjur* and *Tenjur*. Containing 4,832 separate treatises, these editions are great repositories of Indian wisdom preserved in Tibetan translation – and in many cases the original versions do not survive. In addition, over the centuries the four main schools of Tibetan Buddhism have produced their own vast library of religious writings.

Tibetan Buddhism is notable for its great array of deities, which are understood as manifestations of aspects of the psyche and as such are invoked in Tantric practice in order to overcome mental obstacles that stand in the way of awakening. Shown here is Mahakala, one of the wrathful deities known as "Dharma protectors" (see pages 74–77).

This deep probing led Mahayana Buddhists to posit two distinct levels of "truth": "conventional truth" (the table is an independent entity) and "ultimate truth" (the table has no independent existence). With a correct understanding (*prajnya*) of the nature of phenomena, such as that possessed by a Buddha, one ceased to grasp after conventional truth.

Essential to the development of understanding is the direct insight into the nature of the self, or ego. Correctly understood, the self will also be seen to lack any form of intrinsic existence – this is the doctrine of *anatman* ("not-self" or "no-self"). This insight will lead to the lessening, and ultimate eradication, of egotistical behaviour and desire or "craving" (*trishna*). An understanding of "emptiness" is thus the antidote to the craving that gives rise to *duhkha* (see box on page 29).

During the early phase of the diffusion of Buddhism in Tibet, many Mahayana teachers visited the country from India and China. The Buddhism that they brought ranged from the philosophy and logic of a teacher such as Shantarakshita to the esoteric Tantric forms brought by Padmasambhava. There were also Chinese monks of the Chan school – the form that later became Zen. For the Chan school, awakening could occur with a spontaneous or sudden insight, but Indian teachers maintained that awakening only followed an extremely long process of purification of the mind. It is recounted in Tibetan "histories" how King Trisong Detsen called a council at Samye to decide the validity of these differing perspectives. The Indians won the day, and this determined the subsequent character of Buddhism in Tibet. However, practices and doctrines probably based on Chan are to be found within the Nyingma school (see pages 44–45).

# WISDOM AND COMPASSION

The Buddhism of Tibet, while being firmly rooted in Mahayana Buddhism, developed a distinct form of practice, also inherited from India, that came to be known as Tantra or Vajrayana – "Diamond Vehicle". The origins of this late form of Buddhism are extremely obscure. However, it is highly likely that Tantra originated in Bengal and Kashmir, where simultaneous developments within Hinduism led to the growth of varying forms of Hindu Tantric practice.

Tantric Buddhism is known by a number of synonyms, including Vajrayana and Mantrayana ("Mantra Vehicle"), and possesses a prodigious and highly complex literature that is really only accessible to the initiate or adept. The term Tantra comes from the *tantra*s, religious texts that detail the esoteric doctrines and practices of this form of Buddhism. They take as their starting point the spiritual foundations of Mahayana Buddhism, with its plurality of Buddhas and divinities (see Chapter Three) and its emphasis on the development of *prajnya* (wisdom, insight or understanding), as represented by the doctrines of emptiness (*shunyata*) and compassion (*karuna*) (see pages 31–33).

Tantric Buddhism in India, and eventually Tibet, utilized rites, rituals, *yoga*, *mantras* and magic as a way of opening up new possibilities of spiritual experience that could bring about the rapid attainment of the goal of the Buddhist teachings and path. The word "Tantra" really defies translation, but it possesses connotations

Rows of devotional lamps at the Jokhang temple, Lhasa. Made of silver or brass and filled with yak butter that acts like tallow or wax, such lamps are to be found on most Tibetan altars, both in temples and the home, before images of deities.

of continuity and connectedness. However, first and foremost Tantra is primarily seen as a practice that aims at the harmonization of "method" or "means" (*upaya*) – by which is meant compassion – and insight, undrstanding or wisdom (*prajnya*). Compassion is a means by which one gains awakening, but on its own it is not sufficient: the practitioner has to generate insight into the nature of reality as well.

There are four classes of Tantra which are hierarchically arranged in order of importance. At the lowest level there is Kriyatantra (Tibetan Jagyud), which is concerned with rites and rituals, *mantras* and invocations to the various deities; it is followed by Charyatantra (Chodgyud) devoted to liturgy and *mantras*, which are seen

## THE BELL AND THE VAJRA

The two most common symbols associated with Tantric Buddhism are the bell and the "diamond thunderbolt" (Tibetan *dorje*, Sanskrit *vajra*), implements used in almost every tantric ritual to represent the union of wisdom (*prajna*) and skilful means (*upaya*). The *vajra* represents the spiritual path, culminating in the realization of wisdom, while the bell is the symbol of the truth of emptiness (see pages 32–33) – the ringing of the bell is the proclamation of that truth in all realms.

The bell represents the Buddha's "feminine" wisdom and the *vajra* his "masculine" compassion and skilful means, and together they symbolize the indissoluble unity of the masculine and feminine poles of experience. They also represent the unity of *samsara* and *nirvana*: the practitioner journeying through *samsara* toward *nirvana* comes to realize that path and goal are inseparable.

as forms of concentration to focus the mind. Mantras and rituals are, therefore, means to further one's progress along the path to liberation. Put simply, Kriyatantra utilizes external rituals whereas Charyatantra makes use of both ritual and internal meditative practices.

Kriyatantra and Charyatantra are followed by Yogatantra (Naljorgyud) and Anuttara-yogatantra (Lanamedgyud) both of which, as their names suggest, are grounded in yogic practices. The third level, Yogatantra, represents a higher form of spiritual exercise and involves meditation techniques which reveal the unity of *samsara* (the world of birth, death and rebirth; see page 116) and *nirvana*. To achieve

# THE DIVINE EMBRACE

The Tibetan term *yab yum* literally translates as "father mother" and is used to describe an image of two deities in sexual embrace. Such images symbolize both the method or path (wisdom and compassion) together with the goal to be realized (the unity of wisdom and compassion in complete and perfect knowledge). The male deity represents the active force of great compassion, while wisdom or insight is symbolized by a female deity such as one of the Dakinis. The inseparability of compassion and wisdom is absolutely fundamental to the outlook of Tantric Buddhism, and depictions of divine couples in sexual union are widespread in Tibetan art.

In some schools, particularly those that emphasize monasticism (the Gelukpa and Sakyapa), the sexual union of male and female tends to remain symbolic. However, in the Nyingmapa and Kargyudpa schools it is sometimes physically enacted, with the aid of female consorts, by those who read the *tantra*s more literally.

this, Yogatantra aims specifically at the harmonization of means (*upaya*) and insight (*prajnya*). The highest stage is the Anuttara-yogatantra or "Highest Yoga Tantra", which involves highly complex visualization and yogic practices that are said to bring about the "death" of the ego. In this process the adept focuses conscious attention on the "clear light" of mind, considered to be the true nature of mind, bringing about a radical transformation of body, speech and mind. It is at this level, what Tibetans term "the clear light of bliss", that insight and method become truly integrated. From the multifaceted images of deities and *mandala*s (see pages 40–43) to ritual objects such as the bell and thunderbolt (see box on page 35), almost every form of Tibetan art speaks eloquently of the absolute necessity, and inseparable nature, of insight and means. In particular, the union of wisdom and compassion is symbolized by deities in intimate sexual embrace (see box on opposite page).

The initial stage of Anuttara-yogatantra is known as "generation stage" (*kyed rim*) and incorporates powerful visualization techniques (see pages 40–43) as well as a profound understanding of the spiritual significance of death, rebirth and the *bardo* (the intermediate stage between death and rebirth). This is important because for a new spiritual orientation to be "born", old attitudes and views must "die". To become an "awakened one" involves the death of the old ego, with all its conditioning and patterned forms of existence.

The generation stage prepares the mind for the profound understanding that occurs within the "completion stage" (*dzog rim*), where the final death of the ego takes place. Once experience within the generation stage has been stabilized and emptiness forms the continuous backdrop to one's practice, the mind is ready to enter the completion stage. The processes (there are usually said to be five) within this stage are accorded physical status and closely parallel the processes that take place at death. However, despite the physical terms in which they are expressed, these processes are clearly metaphors for psychological changes, which culminate in the attainment of buddhahood, the moment when one awakens fully to the indivisibility of phenomenal existence and emptiness.

# THE SECRET TEACHINGS

The following extract is from a *tantra* concerned with purifying one's body, speech and mind by transforming them into the body, speech and mind of a deity, in this case Chakrasamvara (Heruka). It demonstrates the complexity involved in Tantric visualization practice and illustrates the highly elusive *sandhya bhashya* ("twilight language") in which Tantric teachings are written. After preliminary practices that include the taking of refuge and purifying the place of meditation, the practitioner begins the process of generating Chakrasamvara and his consort, Vajravarahi, at the centre of their *mandala*:

*"Everything is emptiness out of emptiness.*

The light radiates from the *HE* at the top of my head, the *RU* on my neck, and the *KA* on my heart. From these syllables the light radiates forth and touches all beings awakening in them their innate Buddha-nature, and places them in the three gates of the path to deliverance.

For *HE* is the lack of causelessness of all events, *RU* is the impermanence of all events, *KA* is the homelessness of all events. Compassion is awakened in me when I recollect these things and I think: it is because of ignorance of such things that beings are reborn into the world; may all beings become aware of them when I become Lord Heruka.

OM! I am pure of intrinsic-being, and pure of intrinsic-being are all things!

Both I and the three syllables transform into *OM,* and above that into *AH,* and above that into *HUM.* Light shines forth from these three syllables causing the whole world of both animate and inanimate objects to melt into light, and all light is collected and dissolved back into the syllables.

And then the *OM* dissolves upward into the *AH,* and the *AH* in turn into the *HUM,* and the *U*-vowel into the *HA,* and the *HA* into the headstroke, and the headstroke into the crescent, and the crescent into the dot; and the dot dissolves into pure sound. It is from the pure sound that the *mantra OM* is born. I am of the very essence of emptiness, which is indeed the supreme Vajra knowledge!..."

# THE CIRCLE OF THE COSMOS

The meditation techniques of the first stage of Anuttara-yogatantra, the highest form of Tantric practice (see pages 36–37), rely heavily on the imaginative capacity of the individual and require an engagement with complex visualization techniques that seek to bring into being an imaginary world. By making this leap of imagination, the practitioner learns to visualize the world as a *mandala* (Tibetan *kyil khor*), a divine palace inhabited by gods and goddesses, and thus re-orientates his or her view of the ordinary world of things and objects. In other words, the meditator engages in a vivid pictorial meditation designed to bring about a radical mental transformation that shifts the basis of action and thought from a focus on the ego to a focus on wisdom and compassion.

However, an ever-present awareness of emptiness (*shunyata*; see pages 32–33) is considered to be of vital importance in ensuring that the *mandala* fantasy does not tip over into madness. Tantric theorists continually stress that the *mandala*s and the deities that populate them are nothing but emanations of emptiness and therefore lacking in intrinsic existence.

In simple terms, the meditations surrounding the use of *mandala*s can be seen as highly elaborate imaginative fantasies, skilful and wholesome but fantasies nonetheless, that are aimed at the attainment of awakening. Meditations on the deities and the various *mandala*s can be seen as lying at the very heart of Tantric practice.

Above all the *mandala*, and the deities which inhabit it, are multifaceted symbols that abound with meaning for the meditator. They are manifestations of the meditator's mind and have no independent reality distinct from that mind. Therefore the deities evoked in Tantric practice must never be understood as "real" or actual physical beings. The visualizations of deities that arise in Tantric meditation are all conceived to be images of insight and compassion, the supreme qualities that the meditator wishes to integrate into his or her own being. The meditator does this by

# THE KALACHAKRA MANDALA

In the Kalachakra Mandala (below right), a number of circles are shown enclosing a square, which depicts a celestial jewelled palace, the abode of the deities. The outermost circle, in five colours, symbolizes a ring of fire that is said to deny the uninitiated access to the mysteries within the *mandala*. The flames are also said to symbolize the fiery consciousness that consumes spiritual hindrances to the truth. Within this, there is a second circle, usually blue-black, containing diamantine thunderbolts (*vajra*s) symbolizing the indestructibility of the mind and its true wisdom or insight which, like the diamond, cuts through everything – specifically the bonds of ignorance (*avidya*). In most *mandala*s, the *vajra*s enclose a circle of lotus petals, which represent the unfolding of a gentle and harmonious spiritual vision accessible only to the mind cleansed of defilements.

The sacred area within the circles is the *mandala* proper and represents the palace of the deities, which has four gateways at the cardinal points and is conceived in the form of a double-*vajra*. The palace walls are of five colours and decorated with many auspicious symbols.

Within the walls of the palace, the ground is divided into four coloured triangles: white represents gentleness; red magnificence and dignity; yellow expansion and enrichment; and blue-black action. The central area of the *mandala*, which takes the form of a lotus, has another circle of *vajra*s, along with lotuses upon which sit an assembly of deities. At the very heart is the deity Kalachakra, who governs the whole *mandala* (see also detail on page 43).

# THE HAND MANDALA

An image of a *mandala* may be created in two or three dimensions, using material as varied as brass, clay, coloured sand and rice. The best known form is that seen represented on Tibetan scroll hangings, but within Tibetan culture these extremely colourful and highly complex diagrams of mental transformation

are usually found only in monasteries. For this reason the most common form of the *mandala* is a simple *mudra* or hand gesture.

Hand gestures abound in both the iconography and ritual of Tibetan Buddhism and represent either awakening, such as the gestures of the Buddhas and *bodhisattva*s, or offerings, such as flowers, incense and water. The *mandala mudra* is a symbolic offering of the entire universe, with all of the good things contained within it, for the benefit of all sentient beings. With the hands palms up, the forefingers and middle fingers are interlaced, with each little finger held by the opposite thumb. The ring fingers point upward, back to back, to represent Mount Meru, the sacred holy mountain that is seen as the centre of the universe. The whole hand gesture is surrounded by the practitioner's prayer beads (see illustration, left).

first generating the images then, at a much later stage, attempting to integrate the virtues that they represent through difficult yogic practices that involve imagining oneself as the deity.

The highly colourful visual representations of deities and *mandala*s found in Tibetan art are, therefore, inner processes represented in outward pictorial form, as guides to meditation and psychological transformation. It is worth noting that images of deities are considered to be *mandala*s just as much as the diagrams and pictures that represent full *mandala*s in the form of cosmic circles. A great *lama* of the Nyingma school, Romzom Chokyi Zangpo, described the *mandala* as "taking any

facet of reality and surrounding it with beauty". However, the most familiar depiction of the *mandala* is as a circle filled with complex and intricate detail. This version is most commonly seen on colourful Tibetan *thangka* paintings, but it is also executed in other media such as sand, rice, clay and even hand gestures (see box on opposite page).

In whichever way it is represented, the *mandala* is considered to be a sacred image of the universe, boundless and free of the taints of dualistic ideas – a space where deities spontaneously manifest themselves to a purified consciousness. As a symbol, the *mandala* represents the forum or space for social acts of which the centre is the individual. Put simply, this means that the individual can either inhabit the world as an ego, with all the manipulative and dualistic divisions created by that ego, or can inhabit the *mandala*, at whose very centre is an image or manifestation of insight or compassion – a deity visualized as the individual.

As powerful representations of a different approach to being, *mandala*s represent a way of transforming the Tantric practitioner's relationship to the world. Together with the visions of the deities that inhabit them, *mandala*s are symbolic manifestations of inner psychic processes; as such they are created for the meditation session alone and then dissolved once again back into the emptiness from which they initially emerged. For the period of meditation, the *mandala* is conceived as a place free from all the taints of the ordinary world of *samsara*.

This detail of the central area of the Kalachakra Mandala (see page 41), shows a ring of *vajra*s, and deities seated on lotus thrones. Kalachakra, the principal deity of the *mandala*, is at the very centre in sexual union with his consort Vishvamati.

# PATHS TO NIRVANA

Each of the distinctive schools and sects that have developed in Tibetan Buddhism emphasizes different aspects of Buddhist doctrine. They vary too in their interpretation of it and they have also evolved quite distinct forms of liturgy and ritual. The four main schools are the Nyingmapa, Sakyapa, Kargyudpa and the Gelukpa, within which there are numerous subsects. A fifth school, the Kadampa, disappeared by the fifteenth century CE, when it was absorbed into the emergent Gelukpa.

The Nyingmapa ("School of the Old Ones") is Tibet's oldest school and reveres as its founder the Tantric master Padmasambhava, who is also credited with establishing Tibet's first monastery, Samye (see pages 22–23). However, the history of the Nyingmapa is far from clear. With the exception of the Samye monks, most of its early practitioners lived in caves or tiny communities, and no figure seems to have possessed authority over the whole school. Any continuity of teaching was severely disrupted by Lang Darma in the ninth century CE (see box on page 22). Possessing many scriptures outside the main Tibetan Buddhist canon (see box on opposite page), the Nyingmapa differs doctrinally from the other schools and reflects considerable Bon influence, for example in its funerary rites. This probably indicates the extent to which early Buddhism in Tibet had to assimilate and adapt pre-Buddhist beliefs in order to survive.

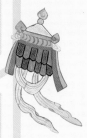

Emerging from the work of the scholar and translator Drokmi (992–1072), a disciple of the Indian master Shantibhadra, the Sakyapa ("School of Sakya") was for around a century the dominant force in Tibet. The foundation of Sakya monastery in 1073 by Drokmi's disciple, Konchog Gyalpo, marked the beginning of the school's ascendancy and Sakya became renowned throughout the Buddhist world as a centre of scholarship, poetry and art. Under the abbacy of Sachen Kunga Nyingpo (1092–1158) the Sakyapa began to develop a distinct doctrinal position. The school places great emphasis on the *Hevajra Tantra*, brought to Tibet by Drokmi, and writings on Buddhist philosophy, logic, rhetoric and grammar abound in the tradition.

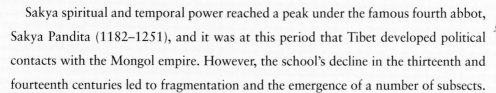

Sakya spiritual and temporal power reached a peak under the famous fourth abbot, Sakya Pandita (1182–1251), and it was at this period that Tibet developed political contacts with the Mongol empire. However, the school's decline in the thirteenth and fourteenth centuries led to fragmentation and the emergence of a number of subsects.

The Kargyudpa or Kagyupa ("Oral Transmission School") traces its origins to another scholar and translator, Marpa (1012–1097), who is said to have been a pupil of Naropa, abbot of the great monastery of Nalanda in India. Marpa's most important disciple was Milarepa (see pages 54–57), whose own pupil, Gampopa (1079–1153), decisively influenced Kargyud doctrine and liturgy and was in many ways the school's true

# TREASURES OF THE NYINGMA

The Nyingmapa incorporate many writings stemming from the First Diffusion of Buddhism, whereas the main canon of Tibetan Buddhist scriptures virtually all originate from the Second Diffusion. The Nyingmapa are noted for their *terma*, or "hidden treasures", writings that Padmasambhava (right) is said to have concealed in various places for discovery at a more auspicious time. Usually highly mystical in tone, *terma* convey teachings often radically at odds with those of the other schools. The *terma*, whose discoverers (*terton*) are often widely revered, can be seen as a means whereby the teachings of the Nyingmapa were continuously reinvigorated. The school also possesses a group of ancient *tantra*s that are unique to the Nyingma tradition, which regards them as the most powerful and sophisticated of the Buddha's teachings.

founder. The Kargyud hold that their Tantric and yogic teachings are the direct revelation of Vajradhara, the Primordial Buddha (see page 60), and must be transmitted orally and in secrecy. A key Kargyud meditational practice, the Mahamudra ("Great Seal"), is based on the idea that the mind is not a "thing" but a natural, spontaneous flow, lacking as it does permanence and intrinsic existence. The largest of the numerous Kargyud sects is the Karma Kargyud, founded by Dusum Chenpa (1110–1193), who was retrospectively recognized as the first Karmarpa (see page 51).

The Kadampa traced its origins to the great Indian teacher Atisha, who came to Tibet in 1042 and instigated the wave of translation known as the Second Diffusion

# TSONG KHAPA

Tsong Khapa (1357–1419), the founder of the Gelukpa tradition, altered the face of Tibet's religious landscape. Like other reformers, he probably set out to introduce a degree of coherence and clarity to a bewildering array of doctrines and practices. In the process, however, he established a whole new school of Buddhism.

Ordained aged seventeen by the Karmarpa Lama, Tsong Khapa travelled throughout central Tibet, receiving teachings from famous figures of all the schools. His religious views appear to have crystallized at the age of forty at the great Kadampa monastery of Reting, where he received a vision of Atisha and composed his most influential work, the *Lamrim Chenmo* ("*The Great Stages on the Path to Liberation*").

In 1409 he established the Great Prayer Festival in Lhasa (see box on page 97) and in the following year he founded Ganden monastery. Only later did the movement based here acquire the name Gelukpa: initially it was called the Gandenpa and sometimes the New Kadampa. At Ganden, Tsong Khapa supervised the monastic discipline of his followers. On his death, his body was embalmed and placed in an exquisite gilded tomb.

His death is marked to this day by the lighting of lamps at sacred places.

Tashilhunpo monastery at Zhigatse in southern Tibet was established in 1447 by the first Dalai Lama and is one of several large foundations that were the power bases of the Gelukpa school. Formerly housing 5,000 monks, it is the seat of the Panchen Lamas, an important Gelukpa lineage of spiritual masters.

of Buddhism. The Kadampa was distinguished by its monastic discipline and monasteries organized along Indian lines. By the fifteenth century the school had been absorbed into the Gelukpa ("School of the Virtuous"), founded by Tsong Khapa (see box on opposite page), which also stressed discipline and intensive study. Tsong Khapa's work was continued by his disciples, including Gendun Drup, who was retrospectively acknowledged as the first Dalai Lama (see pages 52–53).

Central to Gelukpa doctrine are the *Madhyamaka* (*"Philosophy of the Middle Path"*) by the Indian Buddhist philosopher Nagarjuna (second century CE), the *Prajnyaparamita* (*"Perfection of Wisdom"*) *sutra*s of Indian Mahayana, and the study of logic and theory of knowledge. Only when a monk has a thorough grounding in this material is he allowed to study the *tantra*s.

# LAMAS AND TULKUS

Central to the practice of Tibetan Buddhism is the figure of the *lama* ("teacher"), a Tibetan word that is a direct translation of the Sanskrit *guru*. At times the *lama* has been accorded even greater reverence and status than the Buddha Shakyamuni, and among Western scholars it was once common to refer to Tibetan Buddhism by the term "Lamaism" owing to the *lama*s' prominent role. However, this term implies incorrectly that *lama*s are the most important element of Tibetan religion. Tibetans see their practice as simply a form of Dharma, the truth taught by the Buddha; the *lama* is deeply revered as one who can assist the practitioner on the path to truth, but it is this truth itself that is the heart of Tibetan practice, as it is for all Buddhists. Out of the many thousands of monks in Tibet relatively few would be considered *lama*s. Nor is every *lama* a monk – many great teachers both past and present have been married men, living the life of a householder (layperson).

Tibet inherited the central role of the teacher from late Indian Buddhism, which emphasized the oral transmission of teachings from *guru* to disciple. The *guru* came to be seen as a true refuge and an object of great devotion, for it was he who could transmit the true spirit of the teachings and bring forth from the deluded minds of his students the sparks of understanding and, perhaps, wisdom. The relationship between disciple and *guru* is often referred to in Tibetan as *yab tray* ("father and son"), and as a spiritual relationship it is seen as of greater importance than mere blood kinship.

A detail from a *mandala* depicting forms of the deity Hevajra shows either two Indian lineage masters or two *lama*s of the Sakya school. The position of high *lama* of the Sakyapa is unusual in being hereditary from father to son.

A central function of this relationship is the continuity of spiritual transmission. Students eventually become teachers themselves and in turn transmit the knowledge gained from their own teachers. To this day, unbroken lineages of transmission are considered crucial for the preservation of the teachings and of the more profound and esoteric knowledge contained within them. Book-learning, without the teacher's oral commentary, is considered entirely insufficient for spiritual progress and may even lead the individual away from the truth. Deprived of the *lama*'s oral contribution, religious texts are seen as dead things. In the Tantric tradition the *lama* not only passes on the word of the teachings but also, through rites and initiations, their power.

## THE SPANISH TULKU

Shortly after the sudden death of Lama Thubten Yeshe (1935–1984), co-founder of the Nepal-based Foundation for the Preservation of the Mahayana Tradition (FPMT), various signs suggested that the *lama* – who was not himself a *tulku* – was about to take rebirth in the West. A search sanctioned by the Dalai Lama led to a Spanish boy, Ösel Hita Torres (right), born in February 1985 to parents who were FPMT followers. In 1986 he underwent the usual tests for finding a *tulku*. These included asking him to choose Lama Thubten's possessions, such as his prayer beads, from among similar objects. Ösel chose correctly and was officially recognized as the first non-Tibetan *tulku*. His rebirth as a Westerner is seen as acknowledging the importance of FPMT's work in the West. Ordained and trained at Sera Tibetan monastery in India, Lama Ösel resides at the Buddhist centre founded by his parents.

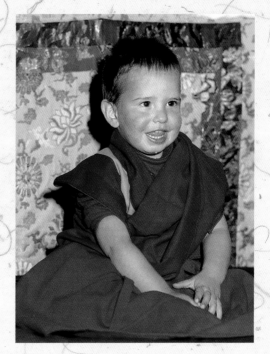

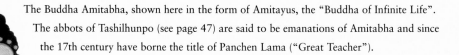

The Buddha Amitabha, shown here in the form of Amitayus, the "Buddha of Infinite Life". The abbots of Tashilhunpo (see page 47) are said to be emanations of Amitabha and since the 17th century have borne the title of Panchen Lama ("Great Teacher").

Sometimes disciples may receive this power indirectly from the *lama* via dreams and visions. Occasionally, knowledge may be communicated through a vision of a deity.

The *bodhisattva* ideal of Mahayana Buddhism – the undertaking to make the arduous journey to become a Buddha in order to help all suffering creatures – finds expression in the Tibetan notion of the *tulku* or reincarnate *lama*. This concept is based on the Mahayana teaching of the "Three Bodies" (Trikaya). Mahayana metaphysics envisages a Buddha as existing in three different dimensions. At the highest level, a Buddha exists as a Dharmakaya ("Dharma body" in Sanskrit), indistinguishable from his teaching of the ultimate truth about the way things are. In another dimension, Buddhas possess a *sambhogakaya*, a "heavenly physical body" that dwells in a paradisial "Pure Land" and preaches to large retinues of advanced *bodhisattva*s. Thirdly, there is a *nirmanakaya*, a "mortal physical body" which, like the historical Buddha Shakyamuni, lives in the ordinary world.

*Tulku* is the Tibetan translation of *nirmanakaya*, and hence *tulku*s are bodily manifestations or incarnations of Buddhas and *bodhisattva*s and other advanced beings who are active in this world with their wisdom and compassion in order to teach others and lead them to awakening and liberation. The Dalai Lama, for example, is revered as a manifestation of the celestial *bodhisattva* Avalokiteshvara (see page 65). There have been female *tulku*s within Tibet's communities of nuns, but there are relatively few of them and they are not usually widely known outside their own nunneries.

In the Nyingma school, the idea of the *tulku* is traced back to Padmasambhava, who vowed to return to reveal the texts he had hidden (see box on page 45). According to this earlier form of the concept, a *tulku* appears only when necessary. However, a later and more widely accepted idea is that *tulku*s appear in unbroken lineages, such as the Dalai Lamas and Karmarpa Lamas (see box below).

Tibet's monasteries had many *tulku*s and a monastery's status often depended on the number it possessed. Upon the death of a *tulku* the search for the new incarnation may not begin for a number of years, since the successor will inevitably be only a child. Often the *tulku* leaves clues as to where he is likely to be reborn.

# THE KARMARPA LAMA

The Karmarpa Lamas, the highest *lama*s of the Karma Kargyud sect, are the oldest continuous lineage of *tulku*s in Tibet, stretching back some eight centuries. The term "Karmarpa" means "man of action" or "he who has mastered *karma*." Like the Dalai Lamas, the Karmarpas are recognized as manifestations of the *bodhisattva* Avalokiteshvara (see page 65). The Karma Kargyud teachings are said have been transmitted from the Buddha Vajradhara (see page 61) through Tilopa, Naropa, Marpa, Milarepa, Gampopa and Dusum Khyenpa (1110–1193), who came to be acknowledged as the first Karmarpa. The lineage of Karmarpas has continued unbroken to the present day, with the installation in 1999 of Urgyen Trinlay Dorje as seventeenth Karmarpa and head of the Karma Kargyud.

# THE OCEAN TEACHER

In the seventeenth century the Dalai Lama became Tibet's most powerful spiritual and secular leader. The title itself was originally bestowed on Sonam Gyatso (1543–1588) by the Mongol ruler Altan Khan, the Mongol word *dalai* ("great ocean") referring to Sonam Gyatso's "Ocean of Wisdom". He is known as the third Dalai Lama, because he retrospectively conferred the title on his predecessors, Gendun Drup (1391–1475) and Gendun Gyatso (1475–1542). The Dalai Lamas are regarded as incarnations of the *bodhisattva* Avalokiteshvara, Tibet's patron and guardian.

Under Sonam Gyatso, Mongolia was finally converted to Buddhism and effectively became a province of the Gelukpa school. With Mongol aid, the "Great Fifth" Dalai Lama, Ngawang Losang (1617–1682) ended a period of political strife and established a unified Tibetan state under the primacy of the Dalai Lamas. The fifth Dalai Lama is respected both as a political leader and as a wise and learned teacher. In contrast, his successor Tsangyang Gyatso (1683–1706) seems to have appreciated secular pleasures more than monastic rigours, and he is renowned today mainly for his love poetry. He may have been murdered by elements of the Tibetan hierarchy outraged by his behaviour.

Other Dalai Lamas who died young were probably victims of the political machinations of the Chinese empire. Under the thirteenth Dalai Lama, Thupten Gyatso (1876–1933), there was also interference from Russia and Britain, which came to

A gilded bronze image of a Dalai Lama, possibly Ngawang Losang, the "Great Fifth", wearing the characteristic pointed "Yellow Hat" of the Gelukpa school. The Dalai Lama wields great influence within the school, but is not its head – this position is held by the Ganden Tripa, or "Throne Holder" of Ganden monastery.

# RULER IN EXILE: DALAI LAMA XIV

In the West, Tibetan Buddhism is inextricably associated with Tenzin Gyatso, the fourteenth Dalai Lama (right). Born in 1934 in eastern Tibet, he was hailed as his predecessor's incarnation at the age of two and enthroned in 1940. After a strict monastic training, in 1949 he assumed full powers early, in the face of the communist Chinese threat. The limited autonomy that he negotiated following China's occupation of Tibet in 1950 ended in 1959, when a Tibetan uprising was brutally put down. He fled to India along with 100,000 refugees; many more followed in the next decade as Tibet was systematically devastated. The Dalai Lama resides at Dharamsala in northern India, from where he vigorously promotes non-violence and the preservation of his culture. He was awarded the Nobel Peace Prize in 1989.

a head in 1904 when British troops invaded Tibet as far as Lhasa. The Dalai Lama fled to Mongolia but returned in 1909, only to flee again in 1910 – this time to India – when Chinese troops occupied eastern Tibet.

On his return in 1912 he sought to eradicate Chinese influence and establish Tibet's inviolable sovereignty. To this end he sought good relations with the outside world, but the traditional religious hierarchy pursued a strongly isolationist policy. As a result of his opposition to the Dalai Lama, the Panchen Lama was forced into exile in 1920. The thirteenth Dalai Lama died in 1933 and his successor, Tenzin Gyatso (1934–), was enthroned in Lhasa in 1940. However, he too fled into exile when the new communist Chinese regime took control of Tibet (see box above).

# THE SAINT IN THE CAVE

One of the most popular figures in Tibetan Buddhism is the saint and poet Milarepa ("Cotton-Clad One"). His life has proved an inspiration to all Tibetans because his accumulation of negative *karma* in his early life did not prevent him from achieving, through discipline and dedication, the ultimate goal of awakening. He was the founder of a rich spiritual and doctrinal tradition preserved by the various sects of the Kargyud school (see pages 45–46).

Milarepa was born in 1040 and his early life was beset with troubles. While he was a child, his father died and his uncle seized all the family's wealth and estates, abandoning Milarepa and his mother to destitution. Milarepa was forced to labour for his uncle on his estate, being fed small amounts of coarse food in return for his work.

According to tradition, when Milarepa reached maturity his mother encouraged him to learn the art of magic from a Nyingma *lama* in order to take revenge on the uncle and his family, who were too powerful to be crushed by ordinary methods. Milarepa studied diligently and eventually used spells and incantations to kill thirty-five of his relatives by causing the house to collapse on them during a wedding feast. The uncle and aunt survived so Milarepa once more used his magic powers to produce a ferocious hailstorm that turned the once-fertile valley to bare rock.

Milarepa is said to have suffered great remorse for his evil deeds and desired to pursue a spiritual life. However, he could make no progress because of the burden of his *karma*. His *lama* told him to seek out Marpa, a famous disciple of the Indian master Naropa. Milarepa found Marpa ploughing his fields and asked to become his pupil. Marpa accepted but for several years resolutely refused to give Milarepa the teachings he requested. Instead he set him a series of severe tasks, such as ploughing fields and building walls. In one particularly harsh test, Marpa ordered him to build houses and then, once they were finished, to tear them down again immediately. When Marpa finally did begin to teach Milarepa, he told him: "I knew when you first came that you

Scenes from the life of Milarepa. Unlike many other great teachers, Milarepa did not found monasteries or temples, or establish a religious order, but lived a simple ascetic lifestyle in the caves and mountains until his death in 1123.

were a very special student, but as you had been such a great wrongdoer it was necessary for you to be purified first."

After his initiation into the practices, Milarepa meditated alone in a mountain cave for eleven months. During this time he dreamt that he had gone home to discover his mother's bones in the shattered remnants of the family house, while his sister was a wandering beggar. Longing to see them after years of separation, Milarepa returned home only to find that his dream was true. Stricken with anguish at the fleeting, suffering nature of human existence, he vowed to meditate in a cave until he achieved awakening or died in the attempt.

For twelve continuous years Milarepa kept to his cave, meditating intensely. It is said that he lived on nothing but nettles and as a consequence his skin turned green. Finally his practice and devotion were rewarded when he attained awakening.

Milarepa's fame spread throughout Tibet and he attracted many disciples, most notably Gampopa, the founder of the Kargyud school. To teach, Milarepa spontaneously composed songs and poems that communicate the intense experience of the awakened mind. They are enjoyed and revered by Tibetans to this day.

# A SONG OF SOLITUDE

While solitude is highly praised as a virtue within Buddhism, it is often a simple fact of life for those dwelling among the high peaks of the Himalayas. Tibetan poetry, and particularly the poems of Milarepa, embraces the pleasures of solitary life and expresses an overwhelming love of the often cruel and harsh Tibetan landscape. In his poem *A Song of Solitude*, of which the following is an extract, Milarepa literally sings of his joy at living in solitude and wandering alone through the mountains.

"This mountain land full of meadows and
  bright flowers is a joyful place.

In the forest trees dance
  and monkeys play,

birds give voice to all kinds of beautiful song
  and bees weave and float.

Delicious summer and winter rain cascades,
Autumn and spring mists roll in,
The rainbow sparkles night and day.

In such solitude Mila, the cotton-clad one,
  finds his joy.

I contemplate the emptiness of all things
  and see the clear light,

Happy when all manner of things appear
  before me: the more things that appear the
  happier I become,

For my body and mind are free of evil.

Happy am I as things whirl about me –

In their coming and going I remain happy,
  for free am I of passion's rising and falling.

In the very centre of visions I am happy,
  for free of passion am I.

Happy in the turning of sorrow to joy,
  happy in my body's strength,

Happy in the triumphant songs I sing,
  in my running and leaping dance,

Happy at the turning into words
  of the sounds I hum,

Happy in my spontaneous power. ..."

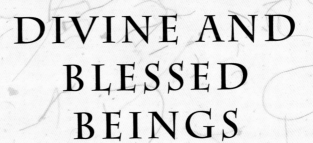

# DIVINE AND BLESSED BEINGS

T he pantheon of Tibetan Buddhism
is populated by a vast array of
peaceful and wrathful deities (*lha*), from
tranquil Buddhas and *bodhisattva*s to
fierce and terrifying guardian deities.
These beings, some of which are of
Indian origin while others derive from
Tibet's indigenous Bon religion, testify
to the power of the Tibetan imagination
to generate potent symbols of metamor-
phosis. Ordinary Tibetans may simply
invoke the blessings of such deities on
their health or harvest, while in the
monasteries they may be the focus of
elaborate Tantric rites aimed at the complete transformation of the individual.

# THE CELESTIAL BUDDHAS

One of the most basic concepts behind Vajrayana Buddhism is the idea of a "Primordial Buddha", or Adibuddha (Dangpoy Sanggyas in Tibetan). The Primordial Buddha is the supreme deity, the timeless source of all the Buddhas and the Dharma, and the personification of *prajnya* (wisdom, insight or understanding).

Within the Vajrayana tradition, the Adibuddha is most commonly known as Vajradhara ("Vajra Holder"), a being that exists in the dimension of Dharmakaya ("Dharma body"), the highest form of existence (see page 50). Seen as the fount of Tantric teachings, Vajradhara is also considered to be the prototype and symbol of the "Buddha nature" (Tathagathagarbha), the potentiality for buddhahood that is latent within all human beings. Discovering and recognizing one's Buddha nature – which is held to be one's own true nature – is the goal of Tantric practice.

Iconographically, the Adibuddha can be identified by his characteristic gesture of crossed hands, which symbolizes duality and the indivisibility of wisdom and emptiness. He holds the ritual *vajra* in his left hand and bell in his right (see box on page 35). However, despite his representation in human form and the great veneration in which he is held, it is important to remember that the Adibuddha Vajradhara is only

The five circles on this Tibetan funerary ritual painting of uncertain date represent the five celestial Dhyani Buddhas (see main text): Ratnasambhava (yellow), Vairochana (white), Akshobya (blue), Amita-bha (red) and Amoghasiddhi (green). Together they constitute the supreme wisdom of the Dharma.

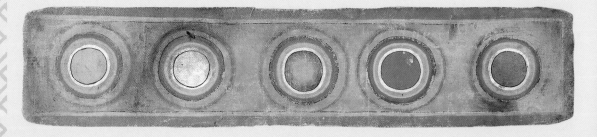

# VISIONS OF THE ULTIMATE

To the Gelukpa school, the Adibuddha is Vajradhara, the ultimate source for the teachings of the Kalachakra Tantra. Vajradhara is equally revered by the Kargyudpa as the Primordial Teacher (Adiguru) and the source of its Tantric teaching of Mahamudra (see page 46).

In the Nyingma school, the Adibuddha is called Samantabhadra, the ultimate personification of all the Buddhas. He is depicted as blue and naked of jewels or clothes, indicating his freedom from properties or attributes – he is beyond concepts or language. Samantabhadra presides over the deities that inhabit the world of *The Tibetan Book of the Dead*. He is depicted in sexual union (*yab yum*) with his consort, who is white and equally devoid of attributes.

The deity Vajrasattva (left), is respected within some schools as a manifestation of the Adibuddha. While considered a *sambhogakaya* Buddha rather than the higher form of Dharmakaya Buddha (see page 50), Vajrasattva is extremely important in his Tantric form, in which he too appears in sexual union with his consort. In this form he is the creator of the *mandala*s of all the Tantric deities. He is worshipped especially as a purifier of emotional defilements, and is central to many Tantric purification rites.

a personification of the totality of ideals contained within Buddhist thought. The Adibuddha is revered within the various schools of Tibetan Buddhism, though the way he is conceived varies (see box above).

Similarly venerated are the five "Dhyani Buddhas" or "Meditation Buddhas", a group of peaceful celestial Buddhas visualized in meditation. An understanding of these figures is a key to the symbolism of the *mandala* (see pages 40–43) and also of the type of reliquary monument known as a *stupa* (Tibetan *chorten*; see box on page 85). Each Dhyani Buddha is associated with a primary sound or "seed syllable" that represents his very essence, and from which he manifests himself, and is linked with one of five symbolic colours. The Buddhas are also known as the heads of the "Five

Buddha Families", the source of all other deities. Each family consists of a group of deities which are all said to emanate from the Buddha. Thus Avalokiteshvara, the *bodhisattva* of compassion (see pages 65–68), is an emanation of the Buddha Amitabha.

The Mandala of the Five Buddhas serves as the model for the *mandala*s of all other deities. The principal Buddha of the *mandala* is the first of the celestial Buddhas, Vairochana ("Radiant"), who in many ways corresponds to the Adibuddha. Vairochana manifests from the white syllable *om* and appears at the very centre of the *mandala* seated on a lotus throne. He is the pure light of consciousness (*vijnana*) and from him manifest the other Buddhas.

The second Buddha is Akshobya ("Unshakeable") and he appears from out of the blue syllable *hum*. Akshobya presides over the corporeal realm of form (*rupa*) and is manifested in the east of the *mandala*.

Next in the *mandala* is the Buddha Ratnasambhava ("Jewel-Born"), who is born from the yellow seed syllable *tram*. He represents feeling (*vedana*) and occupies a position in the south of the *mandala*.

In the west of the *mandala* is Amitabha ("Infinite Radiance"), the Buddha who emerges from the red syllable *hrih*. Amitabha is considered to be the Buddha of perception and discrimination (*samjna*) and he appears seated on a peacock throne with his hands in the gesture of meditation (see also box on opposite page).

Finally, in the north of the *mandala*, there is the Buddha Amoghasiddhi, whose seed syllable is the green *kham*. Amoghasiddhi's domain is the sphere of karmic tendencies or dispositions (*samskara*s).

Each of these Buddhas appears in the colour of his seed syllable and represents one of the five elements (*skandha*s, literally "aggregates") of the human personality: consciousness (*vijnana*), form (*rupa*), feeling (*vedana*), perception or discrimination (*samjna*) and karmic tendencies (*samskara*s). Each of these elements, according to the Tantric path, needs to be purified of all "unwholesome" or negative karmic forces and transformed into forces for wisdom and compassion. However, this is achieved not by the simple suppression of the negative quality but by actively recognizing it and trans-

forming it into its "wholesome" or positive counterpart. The meditator's progress on the path depends on the extent to which he or she succeeds in recognizing these elements and transforming them. The five Buddhas represent the elements of the human personality in their purified form and symbolize the overcoming of unwholesomeness and negativity through understanding and wisdom.

# THE LORD OF LIGHT AND LIFE

The Buddha Amitabha (right) is widely venerated throughout the traditional Mahayana Buddhist world, from India to Japan. Surrounded by countless *bodhisattva*s, he is said to reign over Sukhavati ("The Land of Bliss"), a western paradise or heaven where everything is bright and radiant – it is totally without darkness and night.

In the *Sukhavativyuha Sutra*, the work that is the source of his popularity, Amitabha also appears in the form of the Buddha Amitayus ("Infinite Life"). Amitayus is associated with the "long life initiation", a rite of great importance in Tibetan Buddhism. Receiving this initiation, it is thought, will prolong the life of the initiate, as will memorizing the 108 names of Amitayus.

Like Amitabha, Amitayus is depicted as red – the colour of the sun setting in the west. In Tibetan *thangka*s he is usually shown sitting cross-legged on a lotus throne with his hands resting in his lap, holding a vessel containing the "nectar of immortality". A common prayer at the end of Tibetan ceremonies expresses the wish to be reborn in Sukhavati, where, it is believed, the individual will have an unlimited lifespan.

# DIVINE LORDS
# OF COMPASSION

Indian Mahayana Buddhism is notable in having raised the concept of *bodhisattva-hood* to the forefront of its doctrine and practice, and for this reason the *bodhisattva* was central to the Buddhism that was transmitted to Tibet in the seventh century CE. However, the figure of the *bodhisattva* is not unique to the Mahayana and in every tradition all Buddhas are described as having had previous careers as *bodhisattvas*. In traditional non-Mahayana accounts, a person vows to engage in the *bodhisattva*'s way of life after coming into contact with a Buddha. In the *Jataka* ("*Birth*") stories, popular tales that recount the past lives of Shakyamuni, the Buddha of the present era, he is said to have made the *bodhisattva* vow in an earlier lifetime when he encountered the Buddha of the previous era, Dipankara.

One who commits themselves to the long and difficult struggle to become a perfect Buddha is motivated by universal compassion (*karuna*) – a supremely altruistic urge to help all beings to gain liberation from the suffering (*duhkha*) that besets every sentient creature. In the view of early Mahayana thinkers, this made the path of the *bodhisattva* ethically and morally superior to the path of the *arahat* ("worthy one"). The *arahat*, while attaining great insight and understanding (*prajnya*), was in the Mahayana view solely concerned with his or her own liberation from *duhkha*. (It should be pointed out that the original target of this Mahayana criticism was most likely a school called Sarvastivada, which no longer exists, and which the Mahayanists disparagingly referred to as "Hinayana" ["Lesser Vehicle"]. The use of the term Hinayana to refer to the modern Theravada school of Sri Lanka and southeast Asia is therefore incorrect and indeed offensive, and is based solely on the fact that Theravada is the only non-Mahayana school still in existence. The Theravada emphazises compassion for all living beings no less than Mahayana does.)

The commitment to *bodhisattva*hood, in the Mahayana view, involved a devotion to the well-being of the entire community of humankind and all other creatures. The Mahayana vision was therefore of some kind of universal redemption, a powerful idea that contributed to the Mahayana becoming such a potent force in Tibetan and east Asian Buddhism.

A would-be *bodhisattva* must cultivate *bodhichitta*, or "awakening-mind", which takes two forms: a commitment to attaining awakening; and the actual undertaking of the journey, motivated by altruism toward all beings (see page 31).

## FORMS OF AVALOKITESHVARA

According to Tibetan legend, the *bodhisattva* Avalokiteshvara was born from a ray of white light that issued from the eye of the Buddha Amitabha after he emerged from a session of deep meditation. Avalokiteshvara was given the task of working to alleviate the suffering of all creatures. In this task he is aided by his ability when necessary to take on any shape – a householder (layperson), a monk, a nun, a young child of either sex or even a non-human creature. One legend tells how he took the form of a cuckoo so that other birds could hear the sublime Dharma taught by the Buddha.

Another story describes the origin of the eleven-headed form of Avalokiteshvara. It is said that the *bodhisattva* became so distressed at the quantity of suffering he encountered within the world that his head shattered into ten parts. However, Amitabha fashioned the parts into ten new heads, surmounting them with his own so that he could look out for suffering in all directions and contemplate the different ways to help.

# MANJUSHRI, LORD OF WISDOM

If Avalokiteshvara embodies the compassion of all the Buddhas, Manjushri (Jampal Yang in Tibetan) is believed to be the embodiment of their wisdom. Similarly, just as Avalokiteshvara is described enacting deeds of great compassion, so Manjushri is linked to accounts concerning ultimate truth and knowledge.

Manjushri is revered by all the traditions of Tibetan Buddhism and is always depicted as an eternal youth of sixteen, white in colour and wearing the robes of a *bodhisattva*. In his right hand, he wields a sword representing the knowledge or wisdom that cuts through the fetters of delusion that bind one to the world of suffering. In his left hand, the *bodhisattva* holds a lotus upon which rests a book representing the eight thousand-verse *Prajnaparamita Sutra* ("*Sutra of the Perfection of Wisdom*"), a fundamental Mahayana scripture.

It is common each morning in Tibetan monasteries for the monks to recite a text called the *Manjushri Nama Samgiti* ("*Chanting the Names of Manjushri*") in the belief that it will grant the power of knowledge and wisdom. This is considered so important that is often the first text that a monk will memorize in its entirety. The mantra of Manjushri ("*Om a ra pa cha na dhi*") is also frequently recited in the hope of producing the same results.

The *bodhisattva* vows to practise the six or ten perfections, or *paramita*s (see box on page 31). In doing so he or she is striving to become a true resource for others. As the Mahayana philosopher Shantideva states in the *Bodhicharyavatara*: "I must extinguish the pain of others because it is pain such as my own pain; I must serve others because they are living beings like me … suffering must be ended, and no hesitation is justified." Thus the *bodhisattva* is committed to the ending of suffering for all.

The *bodhisattva* path is also seen in terms of ten stages or "grounds" (*bhumi*), successive levels of attainment that correlate with the ten perfections. At the seventh stage, the *bodhisattva* has the capacity to become a Buddha and acquires a Buddha's special powers, such as the ability to manifest anywhere at will and even in more than one place simultaneously. A being who has entered the tenth stage, such as the popular *bodhisattva*s Avalokiteshvara and Manjushri (see boxes on page 65 and opposite), is not quite a Buddha but from the point of view of the ordinary devotee is virtually indistinguishable from one.

Indeed, a tenth-stage *bodhisattva* is known as "Tathagata", a term synonymous with "Buddha" and meaning "one who has gone thus", that is, completed the path to awakening. So while Avalokiteshvara and Manjushri embody supreme compassion and supreme wisdom respectively, this is not to say that Avalokiteshvara is more compassionate than Manjushri, nor that Manjushri is wiser than Avalokiteshvara: as tenth-stage *bodhisattva*s they both have equal spiritual accomplishments.

As we have seen (see pages 48–51), the Tibetans believe that there are *bodhisattva*s living in their midst who are striving to alleviate the suffering of others and lead them to liberation. Revered *lama*s such as the Dalai Lama and the

The Dalai Lama meditating at his home in Dharamsala. All Dalai Lamas are regarded as the incarnation of the *bodhisattva* Avalokiteshvara (Chenrezig), and embody the fulfilment of an old prophecy in which Avalokiteshvara is described as the patron deity and guardian of Tibet.

Karmarpa Lama are claimed to be manifestations of Avalokiteshvara (Chenrezig in Tibetan), one of the most popular of a number of celestial *bodhisattva*s that have become important within Tibetan culture. The name Avalokiteshvara means "The Lord who Looks Down", a reference his constant vigilance in looking out for suffering. Avalokiteshvara is considered to be an emanation of the celestial Buddha Amitabha (see page 63) and is the incarnation of the compassion of all the Buddhas, working ceaselessly for the benefit of all sentient beings without any degree of partiality. For Tibetans, Avalokiteshvara has come to be seen as the very symbol of Buddhist altruism and compassion. (See also box on page 101.)

# MAITREYA, THE BUDDHA OF THE FUTURE

Just as there have been Buddhas before the Buddha Shakyamuni, it is believed that when Shakyamuni's teachings decline into extinction a new Buddha will emerge to teach the Dharma and usher in a new age of peace and enlightenment. According to all Buddhist traditions, this Buddha-to-be is the *bodhisattva* Maitreya (opposite), whose name is derived from the Sanskrit word *mitra*, meaning "friend" or "friendliness", one of the basic Buddhist virtues.

Maitreya is said to dwell in a heaven called Tushita, where he awaits a suitable moment to make his entry into the world. Mahayana and non-Mahayana Buddhists alike believe that it is possible to visit this heavenly abode and many pray to be reborn there. Even in the current age, however, Maitreya descends to the world from time to time to help others and to teach. In Tibetan literature the most celebrated instance of this was the time when Maitreya took the great Indian philosopher Asanga back to Tushita, where he gave him writings on philosophy and the conduct of the *bodhisattva*. However, in Tibet, the great reverence for the *bodhisattva* never went so far as it sometimes did in China, where his cult sparked a number of messianic movements, especially at times of social and economic instability.

Almost every Tibetan monastery has a large image of Maitreya (Jampa in Tibetan). Unlike most figures of Buddhas or *bodhisattva*s, who are shown cross-legged, he is generally represented sitting as on a chair or bench, with his feet on the ground. This posture indicates his readiness for action, as he awaits the right time to descend permanently into the world. His hands are usually depicted in the "teaching gesture" (*dharmachakra mudra*).

Part of a large image of the *bodhisattva* Maitreya, the Buddha of the future, in Thikse monastery near Leh in Ladakh, a culturally Tibetan region of northwestern India. Maitreya is notable for being venerated in all the major traditions; Theravadins, for example, commonly pray to be reborn in Maitreya's time.

# THE GODDESS OF THE LOTUS

The most popular female deity in Tibet is the *bodhisattva* Tara (Dolma in Tibetan), who represents the feminine aspect of compassion or loving-kindness. Her popularity is probably attributable to the Indian teacher Atisha, who entered Tibet in the eleventh century on missionary work. Tara appears to have been his personal deity and, according to legend, she intervened at crucial moments in his life to give him guidance. It is said that he consulted her before going to Tibet and was told that his visit would shorten his life but would be of enormous benefit to many beings.

Tara is closely connected with the *bodhisattva* Avalokiteshvara, who in one account is said to have despaired of ever leading all beings to liberation. In his despair he wept, and out of his tears of compassion Tara was born to assist him. No being, no matter how insignificant, is beyond being touched and aided by her compassion.

Tibetans often refer to Tara as the "Mother of all the Buddhas" and occasionally as a fully awakened female Buddha. However, there are no major texts devoted to her, although there is a *Tara Tantra*, which appears to be of relatively late origin and is the source of the epithet "Mother of all the Buddhas".

A gilded bronze statue of Green Tara. Like Manjushri (see box on page 66), Tara is perpetually aged 16 and is almost always depicted as a beautiful young woman adorned as a *bodhisattva*. She sits on a lotus throne, her right leg slightly outstretched and resting on a lotus flower. Her left hand holds a lotus at the level of her heart to represent the granting of refuge; her open right hand symbolizes the dispensing of blessings.

Tara has two basic forms: White Tara and Green Tara. Green Tara is the most common form, her colour symbolizing the active and energetic dimension of compassion. White Tara is more commonly associated with long life practices and is represented in a cross-legged position holding the stem of a white lotus flower in her left hand and with her right hand extended, as in the depictions of Green Tara, to confer blessings and realizations.

In addition to these two principal forms, twenty-one aspects of Tara are represented in Tibetan iconography, sometimes all in the same scroll painting, and are listed in a popular Tibetan chant of homage to the deity (see page 73).

## TARA THE BELOVED

The veneration of Tara is one of the most popular of the deity practices in Tibetan Buddhism. She is primarily seen as a protector figure who wards off the dangers and vicissitudes that beset the life of the ordinary individual. However, Tara is beloved by all Tibetans, both lay and monastic, and her rite is performed in monasteries great and small as well as in village households. Together with the *Homages to the Twenty-One Taras* (see page 73), the *mantra* of Tara is also often repeated to invoke the goddess: "*Om tare tuttare ture svaha.*" Sometimes the *mantra* is incorporated in a verse of praise: "*Om*! Homage to the noble and venerable Tara! / Homage, *tare*, to the swift heroine, / eliminating fear with *tuttare*; / deliverer, granting all wishes with *ture*. / The syllables *svaha*: to you I prostrate myself."

# IN PRAISE OF TARA

The *Homages to the Twenty-One Taras* is the single most important piece of Tibetan literature devoted to the popular goddess Tara and will be heard during every Tibetan ritual in which she is invoked. Each verse of the chant refers to one of Tara's twenty-one aspects, which are represented in the *thangka* opposite. The following is an extract:

"OM! Homage to the noble and venerable Tara!

Homage to the swift heroine
whose eyes flash like lightning,
arising from the centre
of the lotus-face of the protector of the triple
world.

Homage, Lady whose face is filled
with a hundred autumn moons,
glowing with the bright light
of a thousand stars.

Homage, Lady whose hands are adorned with
a lotus flower,
a blue and gold lotus;
who embodies giving, vigour,
austerity, calm, patience and meditation. ...

Homage, Lady whose crown spreads a garland
of shining and happy beams of light,
and whose mocking laughter of *tuttare*
subjugates the forces of evil presiding over the
world.

Homage, Lady who is able to summon before
her
all the protectors of the world,
saving all from distress by the movement
of her frowning brows and the sound of *hum*.

Homage, Lady whose crown is a crescent
moon
with jewels shining brightly,
from whose hair knot the Buddha Amitabha
emits everlasting beams of light.

Homage, Lady placed amid a garland of flames
that blazes
like the fire at the end of this world age,
destroying the army of the enemy
In her joyous posture of royal ease.

Homage, Lady whose hand touches the
earth,
and who strikes the earth with her feet,
subduing the seven underworlds
with the sound of *hum* generated by her
frowning brows...."

# WRATHFUL DEITIES

One aspect of Tibetan Buddhism that strikes even the most casual Western observer is the prevalence of images that appear to be almost demonic in character. Multi-headed and multi-armed figures bedecked with garlands of severed heads and diadems of skulls and drinking from skull-cups brimming with blood and entrails – these hardly seem like images one would associate with the Buddha's peaceful message. Nevertheless, these terrifying and wrathful deities are an essential component of the Tantric Buddhism of Tibet. Particularly in *The Tibetan Book of the Dead*, they are considered to be emanations of the mind with no independent existence outside of it.

The wrathful deities fall into two fairly broad categories: Dharmapalas ("Dharma protectors") and *yidam*s, which are personal guardian deities. As their name suggests, the Dharmapalas are deities who defend the Dharma, the Buddhist doctrines and teachings, from corruption and degeneration and from forces hostile to it. It is also the function of the Dharmapala to protect the individual practitioner from all kinds of deception and delusion.

There are two major types of Dharmapala: Mahakalas (male) and Mahakalis (female), both of which are depicted as black or dark blue in colour. There are a great many Dharmapalas within these categories, but the most widely known are Mahakala, Vajrapani, Yamantaka, Hayagriva and Shri Devi. These are complex figures with numerous heads, arms and legs; their various hands carry symbolic implements and they are generally depicted with a third eye (symbolizing the insight that cuts through delusion) and flaming red hair.

All of the Dharmapalas are wrathful, with the exception of a further group known as Lokapalas, who exist in both peaceful and wrathful forms. These deities are also protectors of the Dharma but have the additional task of protecting the Tibetan nation. Mostly drawn from the indigenous Bon tradition, they include the "guardians of the four directions", who are associated with Indian iconography: in the east is

A *thangka* of the Dharmapala Yamantaka ("Death-Destroyer"), opponent of the forces of death. Considered to be a manifestation of Manjushri, the *bodhisattva* of wisdom, Yamantaka is particularly important in the Nyingma and Geluk schools.

Yukhorkhyong (Sanskrit Dhritarashtra), who is white in colour and holds a lute; in the west is the red figure of Chenmizang (Virupaksha), who holds a small *stupa*; in the south is the blue Phakyepo (Virudhaka), who wields a sword; and in the north is Namtoese (Vaishravana), a yellow figure carrying a banner.

Most Tibetan rituals involve the invocation of one of the Dharmapalas, who is requested to keep the site of the ritual free from impure thoughts and actions. Within the monasteries the Dharmapalas have their own temple or sanctuary called a *gon khang* ("protector house") that is used exclusively for their invocation.

The term *yidam* (Sanskrit *ishta devata*) literally means "personal deity". *Yidam*s can be peaceful, wrathful and "semi-wrathful". The wrathful *yidam*s are complementary figures of *bodhisattva*s such as Manjushri, Tara and Avalokiteshvara, who as peaceful manifestations of wisdom and compassion can also be personal deities. Wrathful *yidam*s are usually represented with their female iconographic counterparts, the *dakini*s (see pages 78–79), but may also be represented alone. Some of the Dharmapalas, such as Yamantaka, can also be personal deities. Out of the large numbers of male and female *yidam*s the most widely known are Guhyasamaja,

The major female Dharmapala is Shri Devi ("Glorious Goddess"), known in Tibetan as Palden Lhamo. She rides a mule through a sea of blood with a club in one hand and a blood-filled skull in the other.

Hevajra, Chakrasamvara, Vajrabhairava and the *dakini* Vajravarahi (see box on page 79). All *yidam*s are said to belong to a particular Buddha "family". For example Chakrasamvara belongs to the family of Ratnasambhava, one of the five celestial Dhyani Buddhas (see page 62), who represents the wisdom of equality and the overcoming of pride and self-seeking activity. The Buddha families are represented also by colours, seasons, elements and directions.

To understand the wrathful and peaceful *yidam*s it is necessary to reflect briefly upon the nature of our conscious life. First and foremost, these deities are psychological phenomena that symbolize both peaceful and wrathful forces within the psyche: as such, they are said to exist within all human beings. These forces clash when the balance of the mind is disturbed by the passions associated with greed, hatred and delusion. In Tantric practice, this disturbing and alarming aspect of the psyche is not ignored, denied or suppressed but penetrated, understood and utilized. The wrathful *yidam*s represent this aspect and are associated with something that is known within Tantric Buddhism as "*vajra* anger". This is an "anger without hatred" which destroys the tendency of the mind to stray into delusion and steers it back toward "wholesome" practices.

*Yidam*s are considered to be *sambhogakaya* Buddhas (see page 50) and are generally chosen by a *lama* for a pupil in accordance with the *lama*'s understanding of that pupil's psychological make-up. It is said that one's *yidam* represents one's own particular expression of Buddha-nature, and therefore becomes a means by which one can manifest this nature. What this signifies in practice is that the individual is initiated

into a particular set of esoteric doctrines centred on a particular Tantric practice, or *sadhana*, which itself is centred on a particular *yidam*. Essential to a pupil's initiation into any of these practices is the intense devotion that the pupil accords to the *lama*, who has the highly developed insight necessary both for selecting the pupil's *yidam* and for instructing the pupil on the significance of the *sadhana*s. Under the *lama*'s guidance, the pupil is expected to engage in visualizations of the *yidam*, who in both wrathful and peaceful form ultimately represents the forces of wisdom or compassion that are to be incorporated into the practitioner's own psyche. Such visualizations are immensely complex and involve much reflection on the symbols borne by the *yidam*.

# GARUDA

A popular and widely depicted tutelary being in Tibet is the Garuda (Tibetan Khyungpo), a celestial royal bird originating in Hindu mythology. Emerging fully fledged from its egg, the Garuda is somewhere between a hawk and an eagle, although unlike its Hindu counterpart the Tibetan Garuda is represented as a hybrid figure that is half human and half bird, symbolizing the union of opposites.

In Tibetan iconography the Garuda is most commonly seen behind the head of the Buddha, acting as a protector and devouring its enemy, the snake or serpent (Sanskrit *naga*). The Garuda represents the mind's naturally awakened state or Buddha nature. As a protector, it destroys the "five serpents", the five kinds of psychological disease that afflict all beings, namely grasping in an unwholesome manner after each of the five *skandha*s that constitute a "self". (The Buddha analyzed a person as a collection of five components, or *skandha*s: see pages 62–63.)

The Garuda is lord of the heavens, flying unimpeded in its celestial abode and hence also symbolizing the connection between heaven and earth.

# SKY WALKERS

The *dakini*s ("sky walkers" or "sky goers") are powerful goddesses who are often taken as personal meditation deities (*yidam*s) by individual practitioners. *Dakini*s are represented as both benign and ferocious. In their wrathful form they are often portrayed bedecked with gruesome ornamentation such as severed heads and jewelry made from human bone. They are usually unclothed and are commonly depicted with unusual physical characteristics such as a single eye or leg.

Despite their sometimes terrifying representations, *dakini*s are almost without

exception images of wisdom or insight. They represent the feminine aspect of one's "Buddha nature", and as *yidam*s they become the practitioner's means of communication with the "feminine" dynamic of wisdom. In the Tibetan interpretation of the term *dakini*, especially its Tibetan form *kha droma*, "sky" is a synonym for "emptiness" (*shunyata*; see pages 32–33), while "to go" means "to understand". A *dakini* is therefore an embodied "understanding of emptiness". However, numerous Tibetan writings also describe how the *dakini*s literally fly through the air.

Among the most important *dakini*s are Vajravarahi (see box on opposite page), Vajrayogini and Vajra-dakini. *Dakini*s can appear as individual figures or as

A late 17th-century *thangka* of the *dakini* Vajravarahi drinking blood from a human skull cup as she dances on a figure representing delusion. Her name ("Diamond Sow") alludes to the head of a sow that forms part of her diadem (see also box on opposite page).

the consorts of male counterparts. Images of a *dakini* in sexual union (*yab yum*) with a god symbolize the ultimate and indivisible union of wisdom and compassion that is the awakened state – a state beyond all issues of gender (see box on page 36).

Like all Tibetan Buddhist deities, the *dakini*s are symbols, aspects of one ultimate and indivisible reality. Within this understanding, opposites are seen not as mutually exclusive but as mutually implying each other's existence – a wrathful deity implies a peaceful aspect, and so on. Tantric Buddhism deliberately seeks out and confronts oppositions so that they can be reconciled and harmonized, welding together the apparent polarities of male and female, wrathful and peaceful, unity and plurality.

# THE DIAMOND SOW

Vajravarahi (Dorje Pakmo), the "Diamond Sow", is a pre-eminent *dakini* within a number of Tibetan Buddhist traditions, particularly the Kargyud school. Renowned for her maternal compassion, she is venerated as the source of the powerful wisdom that destroys the delusion from which egotism arises. Vajravarahi is usually depicted dancing on the figure of a deity representing delusion, holding a *vajra*-handled chopper and a skull cup (see opposite). She may also be depicted as the consort of the god Chakrasamvara.

Vajravarahi takes her name from the sow's head of a female pig or boar that can usually be seen jutting out from her diadem of skulls. The sow or pig within Buddhist iconography is generally used as a symbol for delusion, and its presence in representations of Vajravarahi indicates that when delusion is destroyed by wisdom it does not disappear but is transmuted into great compassion. The sow's head symbolizes this transformed delusion, showing that even the energy tied up in egotism is ultimately not to be wasted.

The abbess of Samding monastery in southern Tibet, Samding Dorje Pakmo, is regarded as the emanation of Vajravarahi and is revered as the highest female *tulku* in Tibet.

# THE GODS OF BON

When Buddhism became the dominant religion within Tibet this did not entail the wholesale eradication of the ancient pre-Buddhist forms of belief and practice. Tibetan Buddhism integrated many aspects associated with the indigenous Bon religion, and Bon similarly incorporated elements derived from Tibetan Buddhist doctrine and traditions. For this reason it is sometimes difficult to distinguish the outward forms and practices of the Bon monasteries from those of their Buddhist counterparts. Bon imagery, too, is an amalgam of Buddhist and pre-Buddhist elements and it is difficult to distinguish between Bon and Buddhist iconography.

Despite its borrowings from Buddhism, Bon has continued to retain a distinct religious identity – the difference between the two religious traditions lies in matters of doctrine rather than outward forms. The ancient Bon religion varied considerably from province to province and appears to have begun as a mixture of shamanism and popular folk beliefs, probably originating in the western highlands of Tibet, in a province known as Zhangzhung. Possessing a vast pantheon of peaceful and wrathful deities, local gods, spirits and demons, it also combined ancestor worship with the invocation of spirits and the exorcism of demons. To this day, even among Tibetans who would consider themselves firmly Buddhist, illness is often associated with possession by evil demons, requiring treatment by "exorcism".

According to the mythology surrounding the arrival of Buddhism in Tibet, many Bon demons and deities were defeated by Padmasambhava, who eventually enlisted them in the Buddhist cause as "Dharma protectors" (see pages 22–23). Practitioners of Bon claim that many esoteric aspects of Tibetan Buddhism represent a primitive Bon understanding of the universe; however, it is quite clear that the most esoteric aspect of all – Tantra – is entirely of Indian origin.

Many of the Bon deities were dreaded and revered in equal proportion as the animating forces behind earth, rocks, mountains and trees. Some deities were responsible for disasters, such as the many-eyed scorpion deity who poisoned small children. There were also the dangerous snake or serpent spirits (*lu*) that were said to inhabit rivers, lakes and other damp places. Over the centuries, the *lu* have been incorporated into the Indian-derived cult of the *naga*s (see box on page 77) to such an extent that the two have become firmly identified.

One god shared by Buddhists and Bon alike is the protector deity Damchen Dorje Lekpa. Clearly of Bon origin, he is revered as the guardian of blacksmiths and is depicted virtually identically by both traditions as semi-wrathful and riding a goat. He wears a wide-brimmed hat and holds a hammer (or sometimes a *vajra*) in his right hand and a bellows in his left. Padmasambhava is said to have bound Damchen Dorje Lekpa by oath, together with 360 of his companions, to protect the *terma*, or "hidden treasures", until the right time for their discovery (see box on page 45).

In the practices of ordinary Tibetans, the three strands of Tibetan religion – Buddhism, Bon and folk belief – overlap to produce an extremely rich religious culture. This melding, and the vast plethora of deities associated with each strand, has led most Tibetans to blur the distinctions between the different traditions. The consequence has been a lack of antagonism among the diverse factions of the Tibetan religious world. Possibly greater hostility has been exhibited among the various schools of Tibetan Buddhism than between Buddhism and the older traditions.

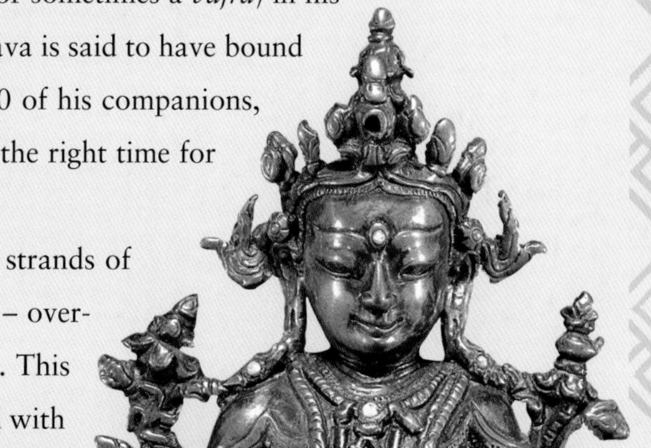

A Bon deity, possibly the creator Shenlha Wodkar, who in legend started the movement of the universe with his breath. As this figure shows, the forms of Bon iconography closely resemble those of Tibetan Buddhism.

# THE SACRED LIFE

Religion is at the very core of Tibetan life and governs every aspect of it, both for ordinary lay Tibetans and for those within the monasteries and nunneries. Even the physical landscape bears the imprint of Buddhism: from prayer flags to *mantra*s and religious images carved into the rock, sacred signs and symbols are everywhere to be seen. The sacred life is woven into the very fabric of daily existence. People will twirl prayer wheels while engaging in mundane tasks, and the recitation of *mantra*s forms a constant backdrop to everyday activity. Every village has its unassuming shrine or *lha khang* ("deity house") presided over by a monk who officiates at rites for the sick and dying.

# HOUSES OF ENLIGHTENMENT

Ever since the arrival of Buddhism, traditional Tibetan society has been dominated by the monasteries. At the heart of Tibetan life and culture, they vary greatly in size, from the massive monastic universities of the Gelukpa school to small village monasteries housing only a few monks. Considerable prestige is attached to those who are ordained and enter the monastic community, the Sangha, that preserves the Dharma. Further importance is accorded to monasteries because they are often the residences of *lama*s, who are seen as indispensable guides to liberation.

Monks gathered for a dawn ritual at Nechung monastery, which traces its origins to a temple built in the 12th century. Located about 8km (5m) northwest of Lhasa, it has close connections with the nearby great 15th-century Gelukpa foundation of Drepung and is held to be the dwelling of the protector deity Pehar Gyalpo. It is also the traditional seat of the official State Oracle of Tibet (see box on page 111).

Prior to the communist Chinese takeover in the 1950s, there were over six thousand functioning monastic institutions, housing approximately one quarter of the Tibetan male population. The majority were destroyed in the Chinese "Cultural Revolution" of the 1960s, when most monks were forced back into the lay population. However, recent years have witnessed a rebuilding and restoration programme aimed at preserving these great repositories of Tibetan culture.

The great monasteries are not only highly respected religious institutions but were also, throughout Tibetan history, powerful political establishments, their domination of the Tibetan landscape testimony to their former power and supremacy. Like their

## CHORTENS

A common feature of almost all Tibetan monasteries is the *stupa*, or *chorten* in Tibetan. The *stupa* originated in India, where it was initially a building constructed to house relics of the Buddha after his death and cremation. The *stupa* became a major symbol in every Buddhist culture, and Tibet was no exception. The Tibetan *chorten* is replete with complex symbolism but principally it represents the Buddha's wisdom.

Some *chorten*s are large structures standing within the monastery precincts, made from brick and plaster and often elaborately painted and partly gilded. A *chorten* will often house the relics of a famous teacher and sometimes his entire mummified body. Miniature *chorten*s, made from silver and inlaid with precious and semi-precious stones, are often found within temples. Whatever their size and location, they are objects of veneration. For both monks and laity, walking around a *chorten* in a clockwise direction while reciting *mantra*s is believed to generate great merit.

counterparts in medieval Europe, the monasteries of Tibet were large landowning institutions. This was particularly true of the huge Gelukpa monasteries of Ganden, Drepung – the world's largest monastery (see box on page 93) – and Sera near the capital, Lhasa. Ganden was founded in 1409 with Tsong Khapa as first abbot, followed by Drepung in 1416 and Sera in 1419. These three monasteries were the training ground for Gelukpa monks and the school's major power bases.

Being such enormous establishments these monasteries required vast quantities of barley and butter – the chief staples of the Tibetan diet – to feed their monks. The source of these staples was the laity, who tended the livestock and farmed the land owned by the monasteries. In return for their labour, they were allowed to retain a proportion of what they produced for their own consumption.

The structure of the monasteries varied considerably and depended on the size of the institution and the school to which it belonged. For example, the great Gelukpa foundations were essentially monastic universities, not unlike the old universities of Western Europe in being divided into colleges. Each college had its own temple, but on significant dates in the religious calendar the monks from all the colleges would assemble for important rituals at a large temple that was the focal point of the monastery. The colleges were subdivided into hostels, each housing monks from the same region, who were thus able to communicate in their own dialect.

As large educational foundations, the Gelukpa monasteries also had at their heart a debating courtyard, where monks would engage in a rigorous examination of the teachings via the medium of logic. A further feature of these monasteries were the smaller houses known as *labrang*s that were the residences of respected *lama*s or *tulku*s together with some of their students or disciples. The teacher himself took responsibility for their food, clothing and accommodation.

Monasteries of other Tibetan schools were similar in structure but smaller and simpler. They could be quite large institutions, like the monastery of Sakya, but they were never as big as the great Gelukpa foundations. Tibetan monasteries in the diaspora are constructed following the traditional pattern of those in Tibet.

# SACRED CITADEL: THE POTALA

Sited on the "Red Hill" in Lhasa, the capital of Tibet, the famous building known as the Potala (below) is both a monastery and a palace. It is said that King Srongtsen Gampo built a palace here in the seventh century, but it fell into decay. The present huge complex was begun by the fifth Dalai Lama and completed in 1694. Its name refers to Potalaka, the heavenly abode of the *bodhisattva* Avalokiteshvara.

Formerly the seat of the Tibetan government, the Potala is historically the winter residence of the Dalai Lamas, their summer residence being Lhasa's palace of Norbulingka, or "Jewel Park". In addition to being the Dalai Lamas' winter palace, the Potala also contains many of their tombs. The complex is purported to contain more than one thousand rooms – it is a veritable warren of temples, shrines and storerooms, and once also housed the 175 monks of Namgyal monastery. Essentially an impressive monument to the supremacy of the Gelukpa school, the Potala is vast, labyrinthine and gloomy, as well as cold and draughty – hence the present Dalai Lama's description of the palace as "not a nice place to live".

Halfway up the Red Hill is Devangshar Square, a large area approximately seventy metres (230 feet) above ground level. It was here that the Dalai Lamas would watch plays and dances on festive occasions.

# HIERARCHY AND OFFICES

At the very pinnacle of the monastic hierarchy is the abbot (*khen po*), who provides the spiritual authority underpinning the running of the monastery. He is responsible for seeing that monks under his charge receive a thorough education in accordance with the values and traditions of the school to which they belong, and he also presides over all religious ceremonies in the monastery. Unlike other monks, who line up facing each other, the abbot is seated at the front of the assembly hall on a

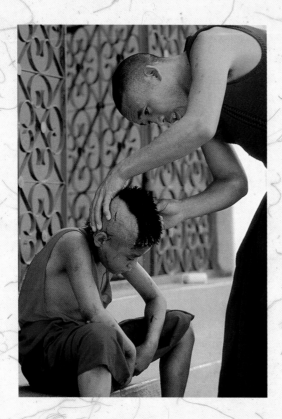

## ORDINATION

With a few exceptions most of the Tibetan Buddhist schools follow the prescriptions of the *Pratimoksha* (see page 90) for the ordination of monks. Only following full ordination, particularly in the Geluk-pa school, may a monk take the *bodhisattva* vows associated with the Mahayana school and the specific vows initiating the Tantric way. However, some schools, such as the Nyingma, do not see the *Pratimoksha* vows as obligatory for entry into the Tantric path. In addition, within both the Nyingma and Sakya schools the vows linked with both the Mahayana and Tantric paths are fully open to the laity. Thus traditional Tibetan society forms itself into a spiritual hierarchy with the fully ordained monks (*gelong*) at its head, followed by novices (*getshul*) and at its lowest level the laity (*khyim pa*).

Monks taking part in a ritual at Tashi Jong Tibetan monastery in India's Himachal Pradesh province, which borders Tibet. A small village and monastery of approximately 600 people, Tashi Jong ("Happy Valley") was founded in 1962 for refugees from eastern Tibet by the 8th Khamtrul Rinpoche, the head of a Kargyudpa lineage.

raised "throne" directly in front of the main altar. From this position he addresses the monks and on occasion directs the performance of ritual.

The abbot appoints administrators (*chi pon*) and their assistants (*chi pa*) to oversee the running of the monastery. The administrators meet together four times a year to review the state of the monastery's finances and food provisions and to plan ways of maximizing their assets – Tibet's monasteries were not just sites of religious activity but also significant economic centres. The lands that the monasteries owned had to produce enough income to support the performance of the daily monastic rituals as well as providing food and accommodation for the monastic community. The basic diet of the monks during these ritual performances consists of butter-tea (*cha*) and the Tibetan staples of roasted barley flour (*tsampa*) and noodle soup (*thukpa*). These basic necessities are held in the monastery storerooms, overseen by an official known as the *nyer pa*, one of a number of administrators responsible for organizing the revenues and food supply of the monastery.

Administrators can be either monks or laymen – it is common to find both in monasteries of the Tibetan diaspora population in India. The job of the lay administrator is to transact business that the monks are prohibited from engaging in because of their monastic vows. Administrators who are ordained tend to be drawn from the wealthier monks – in the past, at least, many were prosperous property owners.

Lay pilgrims prostrating toward monks outside the prayer hall of Labrang Tashikyil monastery, which was founded in 1709 and until the 1950s was the most powerful monastery in the Amdo region of eastern Tibet. The incarnations of its founder, Jamyang Zhepa, rank third in the Gelukpa hierarchy after the Dalai Lama and Panchen Lama.

Monks live under a strict Buddhist code of discipline known as the *Vinaya* (Sanskrit, "Rules"), which governs their daily existence. Most of their waking lives are consumed with religious rituals, study, debate and the recitation of texts. The disciplinary code is derived, at least in theory, from the earliest codes formulated by the Buddha for the regulation of the life of the early monastic community. However, Tibetan practice may deviate widely from these ideal rules. For example, it was once quite common for Tibetan monks, with the permission of their superiors, to return to their families and work the land.

The rules are preserved within a text known as the *Sosortharpa* (Sanskrit *Pratimoksha*) that is recited by the monks on new moon and full moon days. During this ceremony, monks are required to confess to any infringement of the rules. However, confession is performed collectively and not individually.

The maintenance of discipline is important to the effective functioning of the monastery, and this task is entrusted to monks known as *geko*s or *cho trimpa*. Usually formidable in stature, *geko*s wear distinctive garb, including enormous padded shoulders that make them look strangely like American football players. To emphasize their authority they carry enormous clubs or staffs (see illustration on page 97).

*Geko*s are responsible to the abbot for any breach of the monastic code. Those who offend against the code, depending on the severity of the offence, are required to expiate their misdeed by carrying out mundane or menial tasks or they may even be ostracized and forced to sit separately from the main body of monks at religious rituals. Maintaining discipline during the long rites and ceremonies performed at the monastery is considered especially important, and the *geko*s ensure that monks arrive on time, concentrate on the performance of the ritual and refrain from chatting.

With religious ritual such an important feature of Tibetan monastic life, a further hierarchy exists within the monastery centred on the performance of the liturgy. The

## WOMEN IN THE SANGHA

Women in Tibet probably enjoy a significantly higher status than in many Asian cultures, but their position remains inferior to that of men. This is reflected in their position in the monastic community (Sangha). In Tibet, full ordination does not exist for Buddhist nuns – in fact, such a tradition exists only in Taiwan. In some regions the tradition was begun and later died out, but in Tibet it seems that full women's ordination was never established in the first place, probably due to a lack of ordained nuns among the early Buddhist missionaries in Tibet.

In terms of the Sangha, therefore, nuns and monks are not on an equal footing, even if nuns live the religious life extremely rigorously. Today, under the influence of the many Western women interested in Tibetan Buddhism, a school of dialectics has been established in Dharamsala and women now take part in traditional study and debate. However, for the present, nuns in the Tibetan tradition still have to go to Taiwan for full ordination.

The first Tibetan monastery established in the West was Samye Ling in southern Scotland (left), founded in 1967 by Chogyam Trungpa Rinpoche and Chuje Akong Rinpoche, *tulku*s of the Kargyud Karmapa school. It takes its name from Samye, Tibet's first monastery.

figure chiefly responsible for conducting the liturgy is known as the *umzay*, who leads the collective chanting that takes place in the assembly hall. Often possessing an extremely powerful chanting voice, the *umzay* generally holds his position for around three to five years. Upon retirement he retains all the privileges that went with his office.

Important to the status of any monastery is the number of incarnate *lama*s who inhabit it. Although they may have little or no influence on either discipline or doctrine, such *tulku*s are highly valued members of the monastic community. Many of the more famous *tulku*s – who usually stood in a long lineage of incarnations – were extremely wealthy and looked after a great number of disciples.

Not all Tibetan monks enter a monastery as a matter of religious vocation. Many young boys, as in medieval Europe, would be placed in a monastery by parents who found it hard to support an extra child. Even today, children may be as young as six or seven when they first enter the monastery.

However, it is also a source of pride for a Tibetan family to have a child educated in the religious life, and for this reason many families may place a number of sons in monasteries. Boys do not take full ordination until they have reached sufficient maturity (see box on page 88) but live according to the vows of the novice. In addition, not all monks become scholars or spiritual teachers. Many simply serve their monasteries by performing the menial but necessary tasks of cooking, cleaning and conducting everyday business, naturally finding their own place within the religious hierarchy.

Tibet's nunneries are much smaller in scale than the monasteries, and nuns are not accorded the same level of respect as monks; nor do any female figures enjoy the same status as the great teachers of the four main traditions (an exception is Yeshe Tsogyal, the consort of Padmasambhava). There are various reasons for this, the most notable being the lack of a tradition of full women's ordination (see box on page 91).

## DREPUNG THE WORLD'S BIGGEST MONASTERY

Founded in 1416, Drepung monastery, near Lhasa, was once the largest monastery not only in Tibet but also the world, home to approximately ten thousand monks before 1959. It was one of the foremost bases of the Gelukpa school and wielded immense secular and spiritual power – it was the seat of the Dalai Lamas before the Potala palace was built in the 17th century. The name Drepung ("Rice Heap") derives from the monastery's dense cluster of white buildings on the mountainside (right).

Like other large Gelukpa foundations, Drepung was a great monastic university, divided into a number of colleges where monks were intensively trained in Buddhist philosophy and metaphysics. The principal teaching methods were debate, together with individual tuition from highly respected *lama*s, who once included the Gelukpa founder, Tsong Khapa. A monk's training may last as long as twenty-five years before he

"graduates" with the title *geshe* ("spiritual friend"). The highest degree, the Lharampa, is awarded only to a very few scholars each year. Closed and damaged during the 1960s, Drepung was refounded in exile in India. The original monastery reopened in 1980 with a few hundred mainly novice monks.

# RITES AND FESTIVALS

Numerous religious festivals punctuate the life of Tibetan monks and are often the main occasions on which all the monks of a monastery come together. They may also attract large numbers of the laity, who are generally excluded from rites within the monasteries (although they can always visit a monastery as individual pilgrims). The laity are for the most part spectators rather than participants in these festivals, which are seen as a source of religious inspiration, a way for ordinary Tibetans to reaffirm their faith and gain good *karma* that will benefit them in terms of a better future rebirth. Laypeople may also earn merit by contributing toward the income of the monastery by making offerings or donations in the form of money. However, for

## THE FESTIVAL YEAR

The following dates are known as the "great times" (*du chen*), the festivals which constitute the most significant events in the Tibetan religious calendar and are considered important by all four major Tibetan Buddhist traditions (all the dates follow the traditional Tibetan calendar):

**First month:** On the tenth to the fifteenth days of the month are celebrated the miracle of Shravasti and the vanquishing of the forces hostile to Buddhism.

**Fourth month:** The seventh day of this month is associated with the birth of the Buddha while the fifteenth marks his awakening (Vesak) and his death and entry into *parinirvana* (final *nirvana*).

**Sixth month:** The fourth day of the month is celebrated as the date of the Buddha's first teaching or sermon, and is traditionally known as "Setting in Motion the Wheel of the Dharma".

**Ninth month:** On the twenty-second day is the celebration of the Buddha's descent from Tushita heaven, the realm from which he is said to have descended to take rebirth as Siddhartha Gautama.

A giant *thangka* of the Buddha is unrolled on a hillside during a New Year ceremony conducted by the monks of Langmusi monastery in Amdo, eastern Tibet. By the act of making and displaying the *thangka*, the monks generate great merit ("good *karma*"), while the pilgrims and lay population gathered in the foreground earn merit for themselves by witnessing the event and supporting the monastic community.

A procession of monks bear an image of the *bodhisattva* Maitreya, the future Buddha (see pages 68 and 69), on a clockwise circuit of Labrang Tashikyil monastery in Amdo (see also illustration on page 90). The ceremony takes place shortly after New Year on the 16th day of the first lunar month, around the end of February or beginning of March.

the Tibetan laity, religious festivals and dances are often times of leisure and great levity as well as occasions of serious religious instruction.

The religious calendar of the monastic community is governed by the *Vinaya* code (see page 90), which stresses the importance of full moon and new moon days. On each new and full moon all the monks collectively recite the *Pratimoksha*, or code of discipline. Other important dates in the calendar include significant events in the life of the Buddha. The most important of these are the celebration of his birth, awakening, first sermon and death ("final *nirvana*"), which are primarily marked at one single festival, Vesak (Sanskrit Vaishakha), the day of the Buddha's awakening. Vesak is generally celebrated on the fifteenth day (full moon) of the fourth Tibetan month.

The next most important festival is called Shravasti and commemorates a legendary occasion when the Buddha is said to have vanquished rival teachers who had challenged him to a competition in magic at the Indian city of Shravasti (in present-day Uttar Pradesh). The Buddha astounded the teachers by performing a host of miracles that included transforming himself into an infinite number of manifestations, with flames streaming alternately from both his hands and feet. Shravasti is particularly important because it is associated additionally with the overcoming of the forces of evil, with which the rival teachers – referred to in Sanskrit accounts as "heretics" – came to be equated. As the personification of evil, the deity Mara, who tried to tempt the Buddha as he approached the moment of awakening, is seen as synonymous with the indigenous Tibetan religion and folk beliefs, which Buddhism was supposed to have vanquished. In the Tibetan context, therefore, Shravasti commemorates the overcoming of the hostile forces of ancient Tibet and the triumph of Buddhism.

# THE GREAT PRAYER FESTIVAL

In ancient Tibetan belief, the New Year (Losar) was seen as a critical time for the entire country, and exorcisms took place to drive out harmful spirits from the old year. Onto such exorcism rites was grafted one of the most important events of the religious calendar: the Great Prayer Festival (Monlam Chenmo), instituted by Tsong Khapa, the founder of the Gelukpa school (see box on page 46).

The ceremonial expulsion of the hostile spirits and evil forces of the old year came to be understood in Buddhist terms as the eradication of bad *karma* and the simultaneous generation of good *karma* for the New Year. The monastic community generated good *karma* by performing the Monlam rituals, the laity by attending and making financial donations. One feature of Monlam was the gathering in Lhasa of all the monks from the main Gelukpa monasteries, Ganden, Drepung and Sera. This impressive assembly still takes place every year in India, where these great monasteries, refounded in exile, are flourishing.

Falling on the first day of the first month (the first new moon in February) is Losar, or New Year, one of a number of festivals considered highly auspicious by all the Tibetan Buddhist schools. In addition to these "great times" (see box on page 94) the Tibetan religious calendar also includes many festivals specific to each of the four major traditions. Throughout the year, the Nyingma school marks important events in the life of Guru Rinpoche (Padmasambhava); for example, the tenth day of the third month is celebrated as the time when he was condemned to the flames by the king of Zahor. Legend has it that he turned the fire into water while meditating on a lotus flower which appeared from the depths of a lake that he had created by magic.

Within the Sakya tradition, a great summer festival takes place in the fourth month between the seventh and fifteenth days. The focus for this festival is the deity Hevajra (Pelkye Dorje), who is of particular importance to the Sakya, and the recitation of the *tantra* connected with him. A festival associated with the lighting of one thousand butter lamps occurs in the sixth month and celebrates the Eighteen Arhats or "Worthy Ones", early followers of the Buddha.

This detail is from a *mandala* of Hevajra (centre), a wrathful manifestation of the celestial Buddha Akshobya. Shown here in union with his partner Nairatmya, Hevajra is a special protector deity of the Sakyapa and the focus of a great week-long summer festival (see main text).

The Kargyudpa also has its own festivals, which vary from sect to sect. The classic Gelukpa, or Gelukpa-inspired, festival is Monlam Chenmo, the Great Prayer Festival (see box on page 97). Connected to the celebration of the New Year, this is the most important of many Tibetan festivals that represent adaptations of older pre-Buddhist celebrations. Rather than suppressing earlier festivities, which were centred on indigenous local deities and spirits, Buddhism adopted them and furnished them with a distinctly Buddhist flavour, although many also retain elements of their pre-Buddhist character. Thus throughout Tibet ancient beliefs and practices were preserved from destruction by their admission into the sacred calendar of the new religion.

# SACRED DANCES

Tibetan religious dances are somewhat similar to the mystery plays of medieval Europe in that they are skilled artistic performances with a religious purpose. As performances, they are highly colourful forms of entertainment that take place on festival days throughout the year. As rituals, they usually enact sacred myths, allegories and stories from Tibetan Buddhist history for the moral edification of the lay populace. They are generally narrative in character and present, in a highly choreographed form, the exorcism of spirits or the triumph of Buddhism, as in the Black Hat Dance commemorating the assassination of King Lang Darma (see box on page 22). The dances are wordless but accompanied by a monastic "orchestra" (see page 100) that highlights dramatic moments in the narrative.

The most important sacred dance is the Cham, or masked dance, performed at the New Year festival (Losar). It differs from dances at other festivals in that it is an intensely serious ceremony, in which highly trained and extremely agile dancers in elaborate brocaded silk costumes (right) imitate the expressions and activities of deities through the movements and gestures of their feet and hands.

# SOUND AND SPIRIT

Communal chanting is an intrinsic element of the rituals that dominate the collective religious life of the monastery. It is often accompanied by an "orchestra" consisting of a vast array of instruments that includes human thigh-bone trumpets and skull drums, as well as more conventional instruments such as horns, bells, cymbals, large drums and the oboe-like *gyaling*. The sound they produce is generally called "peaceful music", which may seem paradoxical to a Western listener hearing the combined effect of cymbals and drums punctuated by the booming great long horns and the shrill sound of the *gyaling*. However, this sound is meant to represent the crashing of the waves of awakening on the rocks of delusion.

Monasteries often have their own individual style of ritual chant. At the Gelukpa

Tantric colleges of Gyuto and Gyume, the monks are trained in a form of chant deliberately designed to obscure the words and exclude uninitiated listeners. They can also produce a chord – in other words, sing more than one note at once – to create an extraordinary, almost primeval resonance.

Tibetan chant often has strong rhythms emphasized by the large drum (*nga*), particularly in the invocation of wrathful deities, where the stamping chant rhythm imitates the stamping of the deities' feet. The invocation of peaceful deities involves more lilting melodies.

Every liturgy is accompanied by the recitation and chant-

A Tibetan monk at Arya Ghat, Kathmandu, chants to the accompaniment of a drum and ritual bell (see box on page 35). Traditional Tibetan daily life, both lay and monastic, individual and communal, is permeated by the sounds of sacred music, *mantra*s and prayers.

# THE JEWEL IN THE LOTUS

The most common *mantra* in Tibet is that of Avalokiteshvara, the deity of compassion: *Om mani padme hum*, pronounced by Tibetans as *Om mani peme hung* (like most *mantra*s it is in the Indian sacred language of Sanskrit). It is found carved on rocks and stones (right) and even, in enormous letters, on the sides of mountains.

The literal rendering of the *mantra* might be "The jewel (*mani*) in the lotus (*padme*)", the syllables *om* and *hum* being untranslatable (*om*, correctly uttered as the three sounds *a-u-m*, is believed to be the primal sound of the universe). However, literal translations of *mantra*s tell us very little and they can only really be understood when placed in the context of

experience and practice. Nevertheless, the term *mani* probably indicates "that which is precious" – the Buddha, Dharma and Sangha – while *padme* stands for the "flowering" of these principles in the consciousness of the individual.

ing of *mantra*s. These are neither prayers nor incantations, but essentially a means to keep the mind focused and aware, whatever task is being engaged in – one meaning of *mantra* is "mind-protection". *Mantra*s are "words of power", beyond conceptualization. The power resides in their esoteric nature – the literal sense of the words is very much secondary. *Mantra* recitation is extremely common among both laity and monastics and it is not unusual to see ordinary Tibetans repeating short *mantra*s such as *Om mani padme hum* (see box above) while going about their daily tasks. *Mantra*s can be employed for almost any purpose, from purifying the place of ritual, invoking a deity and blessing offerings or the rosary (see page 104), to washing, prostrating – and even going to the toilet.

THE SACRED LIFE

# OFFERING THE MANDALA

All Tibetans know the "Offering of the Mandala" either in its short or long form. In its short form it was chanted and accompanied by the *mandala* hand gesture (see box on page 42). The long form is more complex, its recital accompanying the ritual building of a pyramid-like structure of rice on a base of precious metal. The short form and an extract from the long form are given here:

### THE SHORT MANDALA OFFERING

"This ground strewn with flowers and
   perfumed with incense,
Adorned with Mount Meru, sun and moon,
   and the four continents,
Visualized as a Buddha-field: I offer it.
May all beings enjoy this Pure Land.
*Idam guru ratna mandalakam*
   *niryatayami.*
Thus, *guru,* I present this precious jewelled
   mandala."

### THE LONG MANDALA OFFERING

"*Om vajra bhumi ah hum!*
This is the indestructible golden ground.
*Om vajra rekhe ah hum!*
Outside it is encircled by a wall of iron
   mountains.
In the centre is Sumeru, the king of
   mountains. ...
[On the first level of Mount Sumeru are:]
The precious wheel, the precious gem, the
   precious queen, the precious minister, the
precious elephant, the precious horse, the
precious general and the treasure-filled urn.
[On the second level are the eight goddesses:]
Lady of grace, lady of garlands, lady of song,
   lady of dance, lady of flowers, lady of
   incense, lady of lamps and lady of perfume.
[On the third level are:]
The sun, the moon, the precious parasol and
   the victory banner.
In the centre, all the riches possessed by gods
   and men with nothing missing.
To the glorious root and lineage *guru*s and to
   Maha-Vajradhara and his retinue, I offer all
   this.
Please accept this offering with compassion
   for the sake of all beings, and bestow your
   blessings upon me.
This ground strewn with flowers and
   perfumed with incense
Adorned with Mount Meru, sun, moon, and
   the four continents.
Visualized as a Buddha-field: I offer it.
May all beings enjoy this Pure Land. ..."

# THE SILENT BLESSING

A number of highly conspicuous devices serve as physical manifestations of the ordinary Tibetan's devotion to the Buddhist path. The most ubiquitous of all such devices is probably the rosary of 108 beads carried by all Tibetan monks and most laypeople. It is used for *mantra* recitation and is a way of counting the number of *mantra*s recited daily (as part of his or her religious practice, an individual may be committed to the daily recital of a number of *mantra*s associated with a particular deity). Rosaries can be made from a wide range of materials, including sandalwood, amber, jet, and even human bone. As with other religious artefacts made from human material, this is intended to underline the impermanent nature of all phenomena.

Also characteristically Tibetan are "prayer wheels", hollow drums or canisters filled with literally thousands of printed *mantra*s. They come in a variety of forms, from the very large prayer wheels found at monasteries and pilgrimage sites, to small hand-held wheels that are carried by Tibetans engaged in their daily activities. Whatever the size of prayer wheel, the same principle lies behind its usage and construction. The practitioner recites the *mantra* while turning the wheel, which in turn activates

A Tibetan throws paper prayer flags into the wind on Bompori Hill in Lhasa, alongside a cluster of flags in the traditional colours of white, green, blue, red and yellow. At New Year, old prayer flags that have become faded and tattered are taken down and replaced with new, highly coloured ones.

# THE WIND HORSE

In Tibetan tradition the wind (*lung*) and the horse (*ta*) have become mingled in a way which associates both with the swift delivery of messages and blessings. For this reason, a prayer flag is referred to as a *lungta* ("wind horse"), and commonly bears a representation of a horse carrying on its back a "wish-fulfilling jewel" or *norbu* (right). In addition to prayers and blessings, prayer flags may also carry other auspicious symbols such as the tiger, the mythical snow lion and Garuda (see box on page 77), and the devices known as the Eight Auspicious Emblems (see illustration pages 110–111). The flags are made in the five cardinal colours of blue, white, red, green and yellow, symbolizing the five elements of ether, water, fire, air and earth.

the *mantra*s inside and thus, it is believed, sends thousands upon thousands of blessings into the world. At holy places or pilgrimage sites it is quite common to see a line of large prayer wheels forming part of a "prayer path" (see page 82). As a pilgrim passes by, he or she will utter the *mantra* and turn each wheel, issuing countless millions of *mantra*s into the atmosphere.

Prayer flags work on a similar principle to prayer wheels, but in this case it is the wind that does the work. Prayers are block-printed on cloth or paper with a number of *mantra*s wishing all beings freedom from suffering. These flags are generally hung at religious sites and in high mountain passes and around family homes, and may be strung from tree to tree or house to house. To amplify the message they convey, they are hung so that they are in line with the four points of the compass – this enables blessings to be conveyed to the four corners of the world. When the flags flutter in the breeze or are scattered to the wind, it is believed that their invocations and blessings are activated and sent forth for the benefit of all sentient creatures.

# EXORCISTS AND HEALERS

Alongside the highly developed philosophy and Tantra of Tibetan Buddhism there exist a strong strand of practices that probably have their origin in pre-Buddhist shamanistic beliefs. These include activities aimed at the expulsion of demons, together with those that attempt to divine or even determine the future.

In traditional Tibet, the life of the ordinary individual is suffused with a belief in omens, portents and supernatural powers, and the attitude of Tibetans toward these powers can only be described as one of permanent defence. Everything, including every natural phenomenon, is imbued with significance. This being the case, the control and prediction of the future become of overwhelming importance, as does the ability to read the signs and portents correctly. One manifestation of this defensive attitude towards supernatural powers is the use of charms and amulets to act as protection against malevolent and hostile forces. In addition, enormous importance is placed on astrology and the utterances of oracles – there is even an official oracle at Nechung, a figure who was consulted on significant events that affected the Tibetan state (see box on page 111).

Astrology (*kar tsi*) and the casting of horoscopes (*na tsi*) traditionally play an important role in everyday Tibetan life. When a child is born to a fairly prosperous family, an astrologer prepares a detailed astrological chart that shows the position

An adherent of Chod, an esoteric Tantric practice sometimes called "soul exorcism", in Lhasa. Chod practitioners will perform exorcisms for laypeople by directing powerful compassion at the possessing demons. His ritual instruments include a human thigh-bone and a drum made from a human skull.

of the sun and moon and those planets likely to effect the child's physical and mental disposition. Astrologers are also called upon at other important family events to offer their advice and predictions. Horoscopes are cast when a couple decides to marry or when a member of the family is about to undertake a long journey. Astrologers are also consulted on the auspicious time to commence building a temple or a *chorten*.

Life for Tibetans is divided into events that are auspicious (*tashi*) and inauspicious (*tamishi*). While what happens in one's life is governed directly by *karma* (see page 116), there are other factors at work that may be hostile and evil and need to be controlled or placated. One of the most important magical practices aimed at offering protection from evil spirits and curses is the use of a device known as the "thread-cross". This is made from two crossed sticks that are wound with coloured threads to form something like a diamond-shaped spider's web. Like many Tibetan folk

## CHARMS AND AMULETS

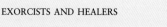

Personal charms and talismans are frequently worn by Tibetans in order to protect themselves from hostile forces. These often take the form of fairly large reliquary boxes that are hung around the neck and may contain relics of a holy person, religious images, *mantra*s and prayers. Among the most common form of amulets are *tsha tsha*, small clay tablets stamped with sacred images that are left in great numbers at sacred places. Amulets are often given to disciples by their *lama*s – they are said to be especially effective against disease.

Much of the work of a village *lama* involves providing amulets and charms for laypeople.

Houses also have to be protected, and various talismans and charms may be secreted in different places in a house to ward off malevolent powers.

practices, the thread-cross probably dates back to pre-Buddhist times, when it functioned as a "spirit trap", catching malign spirits in the same way that flies are caught in a cobweb. They may be placed over the entrance to a house or on the rooftop to trap demons. (In Ladakh, an area that was part of Tibet before being annexed by British India in the 1830s, giant thread-crosses are placed on the mountainside close to monasteries for their protection.) Once it has served its purpose, a thread-cross is taken to some isolated place where it is disposed of by being cast over a cliff or into a river.

Another form of protection is the "substitute", often translated as "scapegoat". This is an image offered to evil spirits as a ransom for a person whose well-being is threatened, and it is especially used as a way of attempting to ward off death. Generally, the substitute is made out of dough mixed with some hair, excrement, mucus, fingernails, saliva, tears and clothing of the person whose life is to be protected. This mixture is formed into an image of the person and decorated with coloured wool, silk and feathers obtained from birds of ill omen. Following a ritual to empower the image it is thrown into a river, thus averting death, it is said,

## RITES OF THE DAGGER

The *phurba* or *phurbu* (left) is a ritual dagger used in exorcism rituals associated with the Nyingma school and symbolizes the ability of wisdom to subjugate evil forces. The dagger's sharp tip represents wisdom as a concentrated, still point that is fixed in contemplation of goodness. The *phurba* is used in rites that involve the "slaying" of a human effigy that represents the evil to be overcome. This evil could be an enemy of the Dharma but also the innately egotistical "self". As a primary ritual implement of the unreformed Nyingma school, the *phurba* is forbidden to all members of the Gelukpa except the Dalai Lamas, who since the fifth Dalai Lama have both received and given teachings on Nyingma doctrine and practice.

A page from a medical manuscript showing some of the many plants and herbs used in traditional Tibetan medicine. In the centre of the page is Bhaisajyaguru (Sangye Menla in Tibetan), the "Medicine Buddha", who holds a bowl containing the widely used healing plant myrobalan.

for a period of three years. A substitute can also be used to protect the life of an animal and on occasions a living substitute may also be employed. In such cases a beggar would be offered a small fee or a piece of clothing to take upon themselves the illness of another person.

Equally common are exorcism rites designed to avert sickness or death caused by malign and hostile demons. In many cases the exorcist will engage in dialogue with the malevolent force after first entering into a trance. In this trance state he is believed to become a powerful deity, which then combats the afflicting demon. If unsuccessful in his attempts to drive away the demon in this way, the exorcist resorts to more powerful magic aimed at the total destruction of the malign force.

Alongside such common practices to protect themselves from supernatural forces, Tibetans also possess a very strong tradition of medicine. In traditional Tibet, the *lama* of a village temple would also often be the local physician; when medicines failed he would often resort to ritual and magic to effect the cure.

Traditional Tibetan medicine is derived from a number of disparate sources. The earliest medical texts show influences from Vedic Indian, Chinese and even Iranian

medicine. Like traditional Chinese practitioners, Tibetans see illness as something caused by imbalances in one's physical and psychological energies. This understanding assumes a deep interconnection between emotional states and physical illness, and Tibetans believe that only a revolution in the psychological attitude of the individual will truly effect a cure. Many ailments are thus seen to be the result of negative and unwholesome mental states such as anger, depression, frustration and impatience.

Tibetan medical texts detail the nature of specific illnesses, techniques for surgical intervention, and the mixing and prescription of medicines. Tibetan medicine employs many curative means and techniques, including herbal remedies, psychology and astrology. In addition they evolved a technique of pressure-point massage that is not dissimilar to the Japanese *shiatsu*. As well as herbs, Tibetan medicinal compounds may contain more esoteric elements, including mercury and even precious and semi-precious stones. In addition to the wide range of herbal medicines, physicians also use dietary regimes to remedy the imbalances that they diagnose.

These "Eight Auspicious Emblems" are widely depicted in Tibet. From left to right: the parasol (protection from suffering), wheel (the Dharma), endless knot (the truth of dependent origination), victory banner (triumph over ignorance), fishes (liberation from the sea of *samsara*), treasure vase (endless spiritual jewels), lotus (compassion and purity) and conch (proclaiming the Buddha's awakening).

# THE ORACLE SPEAKS

Close to the great monastery of Drepung in Tibet there is a much smaller establishment called Nechung Dorje Drayangling – "The Indestructible of Melodious Sound". Founded in the seventeenth century, Nechung monastery was the residence of the State Oracle of Tibet. The monks of Nechung were supported by the Tibetan government, which held them responsible for maintaining daily contact, via the medium of the oracle, with the national protector deity Pehar Gyalpo and his chief emissary, the god Dorje Drakden. The Dalai Lama would consult the Nechung oracle regularly on all important matters of state. To contact Pehar Gyalpo and his emissary, the Nechung oracle would first enter a deep trance, in which he would then proffer advice on matters of state, his high-pitched utterances being written down and interpreted by the Dalai Lama. Upon the death of a Dalai Lama, the Nechung oracle is approached for guidance on his place of rebirth. The oracle (below) now resides in exile at Dharamsala in India, where he continues to be regularly consulted by the Dalai Lama.

# INVOKING WEALTH AND FORTUNE

Vaishravana (Nammang Tose), the guardian deity of the north and the god of wealth, is regularly invoked to bestow prosperity and good fortune both on individuals and also on the great spiritual institutions of Tibet. He is depicted seated on a beautiful blue snow lion, holding in his left hand a mongoose that spits wish-fulfilling jewels (opposite). The following extract is from a common invocation to the deity:

> "*Hum.*
> Protector, who arose from the syllable *VAI*,
> With your great merit you sit at ease
> Upon the lion of fearlessness –
> I bow to you, Lord of the eighth stage!
>
> I praise you, honour you, and bow in reverence to you,
> To your four queens and four princes,
> To your eight *yaksha*s [mountain spirits] who
>    accomplish special tasks,
> To your eight treasure-bestowing *naga*s,
> And to your attendants of the eight classes of demons!
>
> Subdue all the foes and demons,
> Perfecting our enjoyment of the wealth at hand,
> Fulfilling every wish completely –
> Let the aims of others be effortlessly accomplished!"

# THE
# WHEEL
# OF EXISTENCE

One of the essential teachings of the Buddha is that all phenomena are characterized by impermanence (*anitya*). Tibetans, like all Buddhists, have a keen understanding of the transitoriness of human existence and an awareness of the need to make the most of the present moment. To the casual observer, the outward forms and imagery of Tibetan Buddhism might appear to exhibit an obsession with death. However, far from being a morbid obsession, the Tibetan understanding of human mortality is deeply pragmatic and is ultimately intended to lead to a positive engagement with life.

# THE SIX REALMS OF BEING

Tibetan Buddhists have a profound belief in rebirth – the notion that death, far from being an end, is simply the beginning of another round of existence. The term given to the process of birth, death and rebirth is *samsara*. Every time we are reborn, we enter an existence characterized by *duhkha* (suffering, pain, unsatisfactoriness). The cycle of rebirth will continue indefinitely until we attain awakening and liberation from *samsara*, and this is the goal of Buddhist practice.

Buddhists believe that there are six distinct realms into which beings can be reborn (see below). Sentient beings pass through these states according to their accumulation of positive or negative *karma*, a word that literally means "action". Beings cannot exist in the world without acting, and every act of body, speech or mind has "wholesome" or "unwholesome" consequences. At death, a being's balance of positive or negative *karma* will determine in which realm they will be reborn.

Iconographically the Tibetans represent *samsara* as the Bhavachakra, or "Wheel of Existence" (see opposite). The wheel is basically divided into six distinct portions, the upper half showing the "three fortunate rebirths" and the lower half the "three unfortunate rebirths". At the top is the realm of the gods (*deva*s), the highest form of existence. While having no concept of a supreme creator God, Buddhism inherited the Indian belief in a multiplicity of divine beings. However, because they have everything they could wish for, the gods have little motivation to practise the Dharma and therefore it is almost impossible for a god to attain awakening (see also box on page 119).

Those born in the next lowest realm are the "jealous gods" (*asura*s), who envy the *deva*s' good *karma*. Driven by their jealousy, the *asura*s fight constant battles with the *deva*s for the fruit of the "wish-fulfilling tree", which grows with its roots in the realm of the *asura*s but has its fruits in the realm of the *deva*s.

Below the realm of the *asura*s is the human realm (to the right of the realm of the gods in the illustration opposite). This is considered to be the most fortunate existence

# THE WHEEL OF EXISTENCE

The Bhavachakra shows the six realms (see main text) into which beings are reborn, depending on their *karma*. At its hub are representations of the "three poisons" of greed, hatred and delusion (shown as a cock, snake and pig) that fuel negative actions and keep beings trapped in the "endless ocean" of *samsara*. The entire wheel is clutched by Yama, the god of death, who is responsible for perpetuating *samsara*. Freedom from birth and suffering is represented by the Buddha, outside the wheel.

– Tibetans often call it the "precious human rebirth" – because it offers the best opportunity to understand the existential issues of birth, old age, sickness and death, and hence to develop the wisdom and compassion necessary for liberation. A human birth is difficult to attain and there is no guarantee that we will ever have another, so we must treasure this existence by practising the Dharma to the best of our ability.

To attain rebirth as a hungry ghost (*preta*) is to exist in a realm of immense suffering arising from a desire that can never be satisfied. With tiny mouths, skinny necks and huge bellies, *preta*s suffer from a limitless hunger and thirst that they can never assuage. Their realm represents the destructive and limitless nature of desire.

The animal realm is generally described as a realm of great persecution and suffering – one has only to think of the numbers of animals killed for food each day, both by other animals and humans. Animals are driven by blind instincts simply to eat, procreate and defecate, and they are rarely able to accumulate positive *karma*.

At the lowest point on the wheel of *samsara* are the hells, both hot and cold. These are regions of intense suffering, but it is possible to escape them and be reborn into a higher realm (see box opposite and illustration on page 120).

The six realms are not only actual destinations in which beings take physical rebirth, but also psychological states of the mind. In other words,

A bronze statuette of Yama, Lord of Death, who represents the endless cycle of *samsara*. According to legend, he was subjugated by Yamantaka ("Death Destroyer"), an emanation of Manjushri, the *bodhisattva* of wisdom, and assigned to be a Dharmapala and ruler of hell.

# HEAVENS AND HELLS

Buddhism does not deny the existence of heavenly or hellish realms. However, the key difference from other religious traditions is that in Buddhism both heaven and hell are firmly planted within *samsara*. If a being accumulates sufficient good *karma* from previous existences to be born into a heavenly realm, thereby becoming a god (*dev*), this is seen as no escape from the cycle of rebirth. The realm of the gods may represent the highest form of existence in *samsara*, but the only possible rebirth for a being in this realm, once their karmic merit has been exhausted, is in one of the lower realms.

Similarly, beings consigned to the hell realms because of bad *karma* are not destined to reside there forever. It is said that just one good action or thought can propel a being from this realm into one of the higher realms. The Buddhist infernal region also differs from those of other religions in that the punishments imposed in here are self-inflicted – Yama, the god of death, holds a mirror up to those unfortunate enough to be born here and they then judge themselves by what they see in the mirror and are punished accordingly.

the minds of sentient beings continually "rise" and "fall", being "reborn" from moment to moment in one or other psychological realm.

On the rim of the wheel are twelve images symbolizing the twelve links (*niddana*) of "dependent origination" (*pratiyasamutpada*), the factors that account for the movement of beings through the six realms of *samsara*. Tibetans believe that unless the links of this chain are broken, the wheel of *samsara* will turn endlessly and we will experience endless amounts of suffering. The relationship between the links is one of dependence: each link creates the necessary conditions for the next to arise.

The first link in the chain is ignorance (*avidya*) of reality. On the wheel, it is represented by a blind man or woman with a stick. "Karmic formations" or "tendencies"

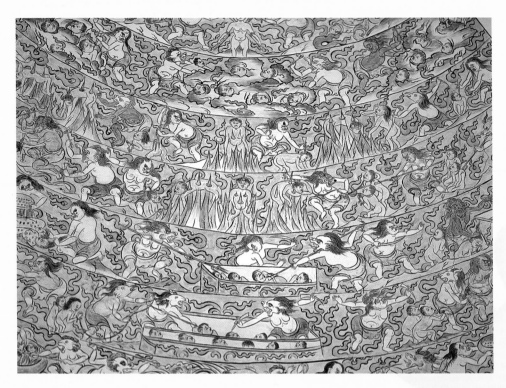

Detail of the Seven Layers of Hell on a mural of the Wheel of Existence at Labrang Tashikyil monastery in Amdo, eastern Tibet. There are basically two kinds of hell, hot and cold, regions of flames and ice respectively. Unlike the hells of the theistic religions, beings within the hell realms are not judged by an omnipotent God. Instead, they judge themselves by what they see in a mirror held up to them by Yama, the god of death. It is also possible to escape from hell by having a single beneficial act or thought.

(*samskaras*) constitute the next link. These can be seen as habitual ways of acting in a previous existence that give rise to rebirth: if our *samskaras* are wholesome we will be reborn in a higher realm, if not we will be reborn in a lower realm. On the wheel, the *samskaras* are represented by a potter. With skill, he will make good pots: in other words, positive *samskaras* will lead to a fortunate rebirth.

The *samskaras* furnish the conditions for the rebirth of consciousness (*vijnana*), the next link, represented on the wheel by a monkey leaping from branch to branch. The arising of consciousness is the essential precondition for the next link, "mind and form" (*namarupa*), the continuum of body and mind. "Form" means physical form as well as all the material which composes that physical form. "Mind" has three elements: feeling, in the sense of emotion; discrimination or perception; and mental dispositions. On the wheel, form and mind are represented by a boat (the body) with four passengers (consciousness, feeling, discrimination and formations).

With the arising of the body and mind there now arise the "six senses" (*sadayatana*), the five physical senses plus the mind itself, which is considered to be another sense organ. This link is represented by an empty house with six windows – the "emptiness" indicating the non-existence of self. The senses provide the conditions for "contact" (*sparsha*). A sense of smell, for example, is the condition for the perception of odours. On the wheel, contact is depicted by a man and woman in sexual union, the embrace showing the close relationship between contact and the senses.

When contact occurs, "feeling" (*vedana*), in the physical sense, automatically arises. On the wheel it is vividly represented by a man with an arrow in his eye.

Physical sensation is the necessary condition for the next link, craving or desire (*trshna*) – if we experience a pleasant feeling, the desire for more is almost inevitable. On the wheel, craving is represented by a woman serving a drink to a man, a reference to the literal meaning of the Sanskrit *trshna* ("thirst").

Once craving has arisen, "attachment" (*upadana*) is invariably the consequence. There are four types of attachment: attachment to sensual pleasure; attachment to groundless views or opinions; attachment to doctrines of eternalism; attachment to prescriptive ethics and rituals. On the wheel, *upadana* is represented by a man picking fruit, again a reference to its literal meaning of "grasping" or "holding tight".

Craving and attachment lead to a desire for "becoming" (*bhava*) and are thus the necessary condition for rebirth into one of the six realms. Becoming is represented on the wheel by a pregnant woman. The desire for continued existence leads to actual birth (*jati*), the eleventh link, represented by a woman giving birth. Birth is the condition for the eventual arising of old age and death (*jaramarana*) with their attendant suffering. They are represented by a man carrying a corpse to the charnel ground.

# OFFERINGS TO THE SKY

The origins of the funeral rites of Tibet are extremely ancient, most dating back before the advent of Buddhism. While the arrival of the new religion saw the emergence of other practices, such as cremation, many of the indigenous rites continued and acquired a Buddhist rationale. A good example of this is "sky burial", the act of butchering corpses for vultures and other creatures to devour. Its origins almost certainly predate Buddhism and its original significance has been lost, but Buddhists see it as an individual's last compassionate act, providing sustenance for other creatures.

Tibetans dispose of their dead in a variety of ways that differ from region to region depending on local conditions. Firewood is often too scarce for cremation and the

A "sky burial" ground, where corpses are dismembered and fed to vultures as a last act of compassion on the part of the deceased. The entire body must be disposed of, so any remaining scraps are cremated. Those who perform sky burials receive food and drink from the family and relatives by way of payment.

# DANCING LORDS OF DEATH

A pair of grinning, dancing skeletons known as *chitipati*s ("Rulers of the Funeral Ground") commonly appear in Tibetan iconography as symbols of the triumphant "dance of death". The *chitipati*s, one male and one female, represent impermanence and are a reminder of the end of all existence. Often depicted at the bottom of *thangka*s devoted to the wrathful deities, the *chitipati*s are shown dancing on a dead body within the charnel grounds where sky burials are performed (see main text), which are often inhabited by creatures devouring corpses.

Masked dancers dressed as *chitipati*s play an important role in sacred dances during the great religious festivals. Their presence is a reminder not to waste our "precious human birth", because death may come upon us at any time.

ground too solid for interment, so sky burial is the most common funerary practice in traditional Tibet and is used for the majority of ordinary people. After death, the body is wrapped in white cloth and laid out at home for three to five days, during which time monks chant the *Bardo Thodol* (*Tibetan Book of the Dead*; see pages 130–133) to ensure a good future rebirth. During this period, friends and relatives bring traditional gifts of barley beer (*chang*), butter and incense for the family, and a white silk scarf (*khatag*) for the deceased.

To facilitate a quick and easy rebirth for the consciousness of the deceased, the family is not allowed to express grief in the house immediately after a death because this might "lure" the consciousness to remain bound to its old home and family. For the same reason, all the family are prohibited from washing their faces, combing their

It is said that before King Gri Gum, burial in the ground or in a tomb was unknown and that kings upon death simply ascended to the heavens (see page 17). By the period of King Lhatho Thori in the 3rd century BCE (see page 18), tomb burial was common for royalty. The Chongye valley (left) is the site of many tombs of rulers of the Yarlung dynasty that unified Tibet in the 7th century CE. These include King Srongtsen Gampo, who is credited with encouraging the introduction of Buddhism to Tibet (see pages 20–21).

hair, wearing jewelry or speaking aloud. Mirrors are hidden or turned to the wall in case the disembodied consciousness should catch sight of itself. Neighbours are expected to refrain from frivolous behaviour such as singing or dancing.

After the body has lain in the house for the prescribed number of days an auspicious time is chosen for the funeral, which usually commences before dawn. All the family are expected to attend the funeral but only one or two close family friends will actually witness the sky burial. The heir of the deceased bears the corpse to the door of the house on his back and from the doorway it is carried to the "burial" site by the person responsible for the funeral proceedings. The corpse is laid out, commonly on a flat rock platform some height above the ground, and a fire of cypress, pine and juniper wood is lit. The smoke from the fire and barley flour (*tsampa*) sprinkled onto the flames are intended to summon the sacred vultures that will devour the corpse.

A small group of men whose primary occupation is the disposal of the dead then dissect the corpse, starting with the back. They lay the pieces of flesh in a heap. When all the flesh is cut from the body, the bones are crushed and mixed with barley flour, which is then given to the waiting vultures. Finally, the flesh too is fed to the vultures.

Water burial, another practice that is probably of pre-Buddhist origin, is used for disposing of the bodies of beggars and the very poor. The body is taken to a river bank, dismembered and thrown into the water, or sometimes swathed in a cloth and thrown in whole. Those who die of contagious illnesses are interred, as are murderers and other serious criminals, to whom sky burial is forbidden. It is popularly believed that burial will trap the consciousness of a criminal underground and prevent it from being reborn, thus eventually bringing about the extinction of criminals.

Cremation is generally reserved for scholars and monks. The bodies are burned and the ashes scattered to the winds or, in the case of highly revered *lama*s, placed within a *stupa* (*chorten*). Sometimes a *lama*'s entire embalmed body may be placed in a *stupa* – this happened recently to Ling Rinpoche, the senior tutor of the present Dalai Lama.

# MATERIALS OF IMPERMANENCE

The overwhelming importance of death and impermanence to Buddhist thought is reflected in the wide range of Tibetan religious artefacts made from transitory materials. Complex *mandala*s are made from coloured sand with exquisite skill and patience (right) and simply swept away after the ritual for which they are intended, and beautiful offerings placed on the shrines are sculpted out of butter. Moreover, human finitude is emphasized by objects made from human sources such as bone and even skin, such as skull-drums and thigh bone trumpets.

Far from brooding on death, Tibetan culture confronts death and then gets on with life. The use of such materials under-scores for all Tibetans the urgency with which life should be approached. A Tibetan motto could be: do not squander today, for there may be no tomorrow.

# BETWEEN DEATH AND LIFE

Unless one has been fortunate enough to attain awakening, death will inevitably be followed by rebirth. According to the Theravada Buddhist schools of Sri Lanka, Thailand and Burma, rebirth occurs immediately after death. However, Tibetans believe that after death there is an "intermediate state" before rebirth that can last up to forty-nine days. This belief derives from an extinct ancient Indian Buddhist school called the Sarvastivada.

## THE BARDO OF DREAM

The dream *bardo* lasts from the moment of the onset of sleep to the moment of waking and includes both dreaming and dreamless sleep. Falling asleep is likened to the process of dying, as consciousness gradually ebbs away. The unconscious state that occurs when sleep comes upon us is seen as the mind resting in its natural state. To utilize the opportunities that this *bardo* offers, it is necessary to view normal waking life as insubstantial and illusory, like the dream state – this is known as the practice of the "illusory body".

Illusory body practice aims to reverse our attachment to ordinary conscious life through practices aimed at controlling dreams, which are merely emanations of the dreaming mind. An understanding of the dream *bardo* can therefore lead us to a profound insight into the illusory nature of all phenomena, as we gradually come to understand that our waking life is no different from the dream state.

This *thangka* from a culturally Tibetan region of Nepal shows peaceful and wrathful deities that the individual may encounter in the *bardo* after death (see pages 132–133). At the centre is Chemchog Heruka, a six-armed wrathful emanation of the Adibuddha Samantabhadra (see box on page 61), in union with his wisdom partner.

The Tibetan term for the interval between death and birth is *bardo*, which literally means "in between". *Bardo* can also refer to any transitional period between two states. Thus the *bardo* can be experienced not just in the period between death and rebirth but in every moment of life. For example, the period between past and future – the present – is a *bardo*.

As Mahayana and Vajrayana Buddhism developed in Tibet, six principal *bardo* states came to be recognized: the *bardo* of birth; the *bardo* of dream (see box on opposite page); the *bardo of* meditation; the *bardo* of dying; the *bardo* of *dharmata* ; and the *bardo* of becoming. All six *bardo*s can last for short or long periods of time and represent the transition from one state to another.

The *bardo* of *dharmata* (literally "luminosity") is the state in which the consciousness rests after death and before rebirth; it has been called a "neutral ground" of pure reality – the way things really are. The experience of the *dharmata* may cause our consciousness to react with fear, which arises from our karmic *samskara*s (see pages 119–120) and a continued attachment to life. Unless this attachment can be overcome, rebirth will ensue. However, if we do overcome our fear in this *bardo* and recognize the state of *dharmata* in which our consciousness resides, we can attain awakening

and liberation from *samsara*. The purpose of *Bardo Thodol* (*Tibetan Book of the Dead*) is to help the deceased to achieve this end (see pages 130–133).

The *bardo* of birth lasts for the whole of an individual's lifetime from birth to death. For those born into the human realm it presents a unique opportunity to take advantage of one's "precious human birth", the most fortunate of all states of existence (see pages 116–118). The *Bardo Thodol* urges people not to squander this opportunity: we should abandon laziness and make the most of this ideal chance to pursue liberation from the cycle of birth, death and rebirth with its attendant suffering. To take advantage of the *bardo* of birth means to embark on the spiritual journey that begins with hearing the Buddhist teachings (Dharma) and is followed by intensive study and meditation. If this journey is undertaken in earnest, it is believed, there is a very real possibility that one will attain awakening and liberation in this lifetime.

The quality of "in-between-ness" is important to an understanding of the various *bardo* states. As an "in-between", every *bardo* is a unique juncture, a point where we are obliged to make a choice. This can be likened to a person standing at a crossroads confronted by a number of roads where a decision has to be taken as to which path or road to take.

A bronze statue of Hayagriva, a wrathful manifestation of the Buddha Amitabha encountered in the *bardo* of dying. In his right hand he wields the blue sword of wisdom with a gold *vajra* handle. On the crown of his head is a small horse's head, an allusion to his name, which means "Horse-Necked One".

A masked dancer at Likir monastery in Ladakh taking part in the sacred Cham dance traditionally performed at Tibetan New Year (Losar) (see box on page 99). The dancer wears the richly brocaded costume of the bull-headed protector deity Yama Dharmaraja, who is identified with Yama, Lord of Death. Yama Dharmaraja wields a skeleton club and wears a diadem of human skulls.

Life, in fact, is a series of often unrecognized *bardo*s, in which decision is constantly required. Whenever one state of mind declines and another arises, the period in between, however brief, is a *bardo*.

While comprehending the nature of all the *bardo* states is central to the process immediately following death, Tibetan teachers also constantly stress the importance of understanding the relevance of *bardo* states to the individual's present life. Such an understanding, they insist, reveals unique opportunities for the lessening of egotism and the possibility of either awakening and liberation or of being "reborn" in better states of mind.

The six *bardo* states represent, like the six realms of existence (see pages 116–118), six distinct modes of consciousness. Mostly these modes go unrecognized owing to the primal confusion or ignorance (*avidya*) and egocentricity that are part of the condition of existence in *samsara*. However, from time to time, the solidity of the ego and our confused apprehension are undermined by sudden "gaps" in which we perceive a degree of clarity. Such moments are *bardo* experiences and present excellent opportunities to effect a profound change in our consciousness. To make the most of the opportunities presented at such times requires a firm foundation in meditational practice, which generates calmness and stability of mind that will enable us to develop and expand our clarity of perception. Thus, if they can be understood and assimilated, *bardo*s represent opportunities within this life as well as immediately following death.

# LIBERATION THROUGH HEARING

The so-called *Tibetan Book of the Dead* is ill served by its title, for the book is as much about life as it is about death. At the time of the first translation of this work into English, the yardstick by which such writings were judged was Wallace-Budge's *Egyptian Book of the Dead* – a work equally ill served by its translated title. The work's shorter Tibetan title, *Bardo Thodol*, is more accurately translated as

*Liberation through Hearing in the Bardo.* Unfortunately, all English versions of this book perpetuate the original translation of the title and lead subsequently to a misunderstanding of the work's intention.

The *Liberation through Hearing in the Bardo* is a work within a genre of Tibetan literature that is concerned not only with the transition from life to death, but also with life itself. Both life and death, it is stressed, are journeys that involve *bardo*s, which are transitional or "in-between" states (see pages 126–129). In these states the mind is said to encounter a bewildering array of peaceful and terrifying images, and the purpose of such works as the *Bardo Thodol* is to act as a step-by-step guide through the various *bardo*s and their imagery. All the schools of Tibetan Buddhism possess writings that deal with death, intermediate states and rebirth, and the famous *Bardo Thodol* is only one of numerous such works. It is a *terma* ("hidden treasure") of the Nyingmapa (see box on page 45), which is Tibet's oldest school.

A manuscript of the *Bardo Thodol*, better known in the West – if somewhat misleadingly – as *The Tibetan Book of the Dead.* The illustrations depict two *dakini*s, who are among the wrathful deities that the consciousness of the deceased can expect to encounter in the *bardo*. Once the corpse has been disposed of, the text is recited to an image of the deceased.

The words of the *Bardo Thodol* are spoken into the ear of a dead or dying person as a comprehensive guide through the various states that they will experience in the *bardo* and the imagery associated with them. Throughout the recitation the consciousness of the deceased is reminded that the images that it encounters in the *bardo*, both gentle and terrifying, are nothing but aspects of itself, emanations and projections of the mind of the deceased: "Do not be afraid, do not be terrified, do not be bewildered, recognize this as the form of your own mind."

It is believed that if the representations that appear in the *bardo* are correctly recognized as aspects of the self, one will achieve a higher form of rebirth, or even awakening and *nirvana*, the desired liberation from the entire cycle of birth and death. However, if the visions are not recognized, the consciousness will simply be propelled by the force of its *karma* to take rebirth once again in one of the six realms of *samsara* (see pages 116–121) – and very likely in a less fortunate realm than the human one.

The consciousness of the deceased is said to dwell in the *bardo* for a period of up to forty-nine days, after which rebirth will automatically occur unless the consciousness has succeeded in attaining awakening. Upon death, the consciousness of the deceased initially dwells in "clear light" for three days, which is then followed by seven days in the *bardo*. If rebirth does not take place

A *thangka* of the Adibuddha Samantabhadra (centre), who is the first peaceful deity to be encountered in the *bardo* by the deceased. He is blue in colour and sits in a posture of meditation, embraced by his consort Samantabhadri. The couple are surrounded by a host of other divinities, including the Buddhas who preside over the six realms of existence.

# CONFRONTING THE DEITIES

Early in the *bardo* the consciousness encounters peaceful deities embodying the qualities of the awakened state. Appearing successively are Samantabhadra, who represents the essence of all the peaceful deities, and the five Dhyani Buddhas. However, the very peacefulness of these deities may be frightening to the unawakened consciousness in that it offers a glimpse of a radically different way of being.

The journey through the *bardo* culminates in a confrontation with the fifty-eight wrathful deities. These are also compassionate, but appear in an aggressive and dynamic form, drinking blood and encircled by fire, and the consciousness will naturally wish to flee them if it has built up no relationship with them before death. These figures represent the intensity, passion and dynamic power of compassion, seeking to shock the consciousness into recognition.

during this latter period, the journey will be repeated and this can occur up to seven times to the total of forty-nine days. In the *bardo*, the consciousness will come face to face with a host of peaceful and wrathful deities (see box above).

However, while the recitation of the *Bardo Thodol* into the ear of the deceased person may help to guide them into a more fortunate rebirth, it is thought that the recitation will have little effect unless the deceased has studied the work during his or her lifetime and in addition learned to recognize the various *bardo*s associated with life and taken advantage of the opportunities that they present (see pages 128–129) – this is what is meant when it is said that the works of this genre of Tibetan literature are as much about life as they are about death.

THE WHEEL OF EXISTENCE

# TOWARD REBIRTH

The following extract is taken from the beginning of the *Bardo Thodol*. The opening passage is recited into the ear of the dying person, and the rest spoken after death. The "Great Seal" (Mahamudra) refers to the understanding of emptiness as the ultimate nature of reality, in other words the state of awakening or buddhahood.

"Child of noble family, [name], the time has come for you to seek a path. Upon the cessation of your breath, the fundamental radiance of the first *bardo*, which has been revealed to you by your teacher, will become visible. This is the essence of *dharmata* [reality], empty and open like space. It is the lustrous void, the undefiled naked mind without centre and unbounded. Once you have recognized this, rest in this state, and I will instruct you further.

Child of noble family, death has now arrived and you should orient your mind in the following way: 'Death has now arrived, and through this death I will embrace the awakened state of mind together with its insight and compassion. I do so in order to be able to benefit all sentient beings who are as limitless as space. For all sentient beings, I will recognize death, at this unique juncture, as the radiance of the Dharmakaya [see page 50], and attain the matchless comprehension of

the Great Seal. I will do so for the benefit of all beings. If I do not reach this, I will recognize the *bardo* state as it is and attain the Great Seal in this *bardo*, for the benefit of all beings who are as limitless as space.'

Listen, [name], child of noble family. Recognize the radiant undefiled essence of *dharmata* that is glowing before you. Child of noble family, at this juncture the condition of your mind is emptiness, it possesses no nature or substance whatsoever. Neither does it possess qualities such as colour. It is empty: this is the nature of reality, the female Buddha Samantabhadri. However, your mind in this state is not simply blank, it is vibrant, open, glittering and undefiled. This state of mind is the male Buddha Samantabhadra. These two aspects of mind are inseparable and as such are the Dharmakaya of the Buddha. Having no birth and death, this mind of yours is indivisible radiance and emptiness seen as a great mass of light. This is the

Buddha of immortal light. It is necessary only to recognize this. Upon doing so you understand that your mind is the Buddha and that when you look into your own mind you are looking into Buddha-mind."

[If the deceased recognizes this first radiance he or she will be liberated. If the deceased does not recognize it, a second radiance will appear and these words will be spoken into the ear of the deceased:]

"Child of noble family, do not be distracted, meditate on your *yidam* [personal deity]. Focus intensely on your *yidam*. Visualize your *yidam* not as a solid form but, like the moon reflected in water, as an appearance lacking substance."

[If the deceased does not have a *yidam* he or she will be told:]

"Meditate on the Lord of Great Compassion [Avalokiteshvara]."

[If liberation does not occur at this stage then the following words are recited into the ear of the deceased:]

"Child of noble family, death has arrived. All must die, so do not feel desire and attachment for this life, for you are not alone in leaving the world. Even if you experience great longing and attachment for this life, you cannot stay, but can only wander in *samsara*. Do not desire, do not yearn. Keep before your mind the Three Jewels [Buddha, Dharma, Sangha].

Child of noble family, whatever terrifying projections appear in the *bardo* of the *dharmata*, do not forget the following words, and advance recollecting their meaning. Use these words to identify what is occurring:

'Thoughts of panic and terror I will cast aside when the *bardo* of the *dharmata* dawns upon me. Whatever appears in the *bardo* I will recognize as the projection of my own mind and know it to be a vision.

Now I have reached this vital juncture I will not fear the peaceful and wrathful visions that are my own projections.'

Advance uttering these words clearly and distinctly and recollecting their meaning. It is essential to recognize with absolute certainty that whatever appears, no matter how terrifying, is a projection of your own mind. Therefore do not forget these words.

Child of noble family, the *dharmata* will appear, when your body and mind separate. It will be hard to distinguish. Shimmering like a mirage on a plain at springtime, it will appear radiant and bright. Be not bewildered or confused for this is the radiance of your own *dharmata* that you must recognize.

Like a thousand thunderclaps occurring at once, a great roar of thunder will be emitted from within the light. Be not afraid or confused for this is the natural sound of your own *dharmata*. You have no body of flesh and blood, only a mental body

of habitual tendencies, so sounds, colours and rays of light cannot harm you or cause death. Recognizing them as your own projections is all that is required.

Child of noble family, no matter how much meditation you have practised in your lifetime, if you have not recognized them as your own projections, if you have not come across this teaching, the coloured lights will frighten you, the sounds will bewilder you, and the rays of light will terrify you. You will continue to wander in *samsara* if you do not understand this point.

Child of noble family, after four and a half days, when you awaken from unconsciousness you will wonder what has happened to you. Recognize it as the *bardo* state! If you do so, *samsara* is reversed and everything will appear as images and lights.

A blue light will permeate the whole of space and Vairochana will appear from the centre of the *mandala*. He is seated upon a lion throne and his body is white. ..."

# FURTHER READING

Avedon, J. *In Exile from the Land of the Snows*. London: Michael Joseph, 1984.

Cozort, D. *Highest Yoga Tantra*. Ithaca, N.Y.: Snow Lion, 1986.

Dalai Lama, H.H. the. *Freedom in Exile*. London: Hodder and Stoughton, 1990.

Dalai Lama, H.H. the. *The World of Tibetan Buddhism*. Boston: Wisdom, 1995.

Dowman, K. (trans.). *Sky Dancer: The Secret Life and Songs of Yeshe Tsogyal*. London: Routledge and Kegan Paul, 1984.

Dudjom Rinpoche. *The Nyingma School of Tibetan Buddhism, Its Fundamentals and History*. Boston: Wisdom, 1991.

Fremantle, F., and Chögyam Trungpa. *The Tibetan Book of the Dead*. Berkeley and London: 1975.

Garma C.C. Chang. *The Hundred Thousand Songs of Milarepa*., 2 vols., Boulder, Colorado, and London: Shambala, 1977.

Hicks, R., and Ngagpa Chögyam. *Great Ocean*. London: Penguin, 1990.

Kelsang Gyatso, Geshe. *Clear Light of Bliss*. London: Wisdom, 1982.

Kunga Rinpoche, Lama. *Drinking the Mountain Stream*. New York: Lotsawa, 1978.

Kvaerne, P. *Tibet: The Bon Religion*. Leiden: E.J. Brill, 1985.

Levenson, C. *The Dalai Lama*. London: Unwin Nyman, 1988.

Lobsang P. Lhalungpa. (trans.) *The Life of Milarepa*. Boston: Shambala,1985.

Lopez, D. S. (ed.). *Religions of Tibet in Practice*. Princeton, N.J.: Princeton University Press, 1997.

Mullin, Glen H. *Death and Dying: The Tibetan Tradition*. Boston: Arkana, 1986.

Nalanda Translation Committee/ Chögyam Trungpa (trans.), *The Life of Marpa*. Boulder: Colorado, Prajna, 1982.

Namkhai Norbu, Dzogchen. *The Self-Perfected State*. London: Arkana, 1986.

de Nebesky-Wojkowitz, René. *Oracles and Demons of Tibet*. Oxford: Oxford University Press, 1956.

Norbu Chophel. *Folk Culture of Tibet*. Dharamsala: Library of Tibetan Works and Archives, 1983.

Panchen Sonam Dragpa. *Overview of Buddhist Tantra*. Dharamsala: Library of Tibetan Works and Archives, 1996.

Powers, J. *Introduction to Tibetan Buddhism*. Ithaca, N.Y.: Snow Lion, 1995.

Ray, Reginald A. *Indestructible Truth: The Living Spirituality of Tibetan Buddhism*. Boston: Shambala, 2002.

Ray, Reginald A. *Secrets of the Vajra World: The Tantric Buddhism of Tibet*. Boston: Shambala, 2002.

Rhie, M., and Thurman, R.A.F. *Wisdom and Compassion: The Sacred Art of Tibet*. London: Thames and Hudson, 1991.

Samuel, G. *Civilized Shamans*. Washington, D.C.: Smithsonian Institution, 1993.

Shardza Tashi Gyaltsen. *Heartdrops of Dharmakaya*. Ithaca, N.Y.: Snow Lion, 1993.

Snellgrove, D. *Indo-Tibetan Buddhism*. London: Serindia, 1987.

Snellgrove, D., and Richardson, H. *A Cultural History of Tibet*. London: Weidenfeld and Nicholson, 1968.

Sogyal Rinpoche. *The Tibetan Book of Living and Dying*. London: Rider, 1992.

Thondup Rinpoche, Tulku. *Buddha Mind*. Ithaca, N.Y.: Snow Lion 1989.

Thondup Rinpoche, Tulku. *Hidden Teachings of Tibet*. London: Wisdom, 1986.

Thupten Jinpa and Jas Elsner. *Songs of Spiritual Experience: Tibetan Buddhist Poems of Insight and Awakening*. Boston: Shambala, 2000.

Thurman, R.A.F. *Tsong Khapa's Speech of Gold in the Essence of True Eloquence*. Princeton, N.J.: Princeton University Press, 1984.

Trainor, K. (gen. ed.). *Buddhism: The Illustrated Guide*. New York: Oxford University Press, 2001 and London: DBP, 2001.

Tucci, G. *The Religions of Tibet*. London: Routledge and Kegan Paul, 1980.

Willis, M.J. *Tibet: Life, Myth, and Art*. London: DBP, 1999.

## OTHER MEDIA

Thurman, R.A.F. *Illuminated Tibet: An Introduction to Tibetan Culture* (CD-Rom).

The best website for Tibetan studies is www.ciolek.com/ WWWVLTibetanStudies.html

Dreyfus, G. "Tibetan scholastic education and the role of soteriology", in *Journal of the International Association of Buddhist Studies* 20,1, 1997, pp. 190-216.

Goldstein, M., and Paljor Tsarong. "Tibetan Buddhist Monasticism: social, psychological and cultural implications", in *The Tibet Journal*, 1985, 10/1, pp. 14-53.

# INDEX

dancing 99, *129*
death 9, *29*, 37, 115, 125
    funerary rites 44,
        122–125
    *see also* rebirth
demons 21, 22, 74, 80
Dharamsala 53, *91*, *101*,
    111, *117*
Dharma 19, 32, 101
Dharma Protectors
    (Dharmapalas) 13, *33*,
    74–75, *75*, 76, 80, *118*
Dharmakaya 50
*dharmata* (luminosity) 127,
    136–137
*dhyana see* meditation
Dhyani (Meditation)
    Buddhas 60, 61, 76, 133
Dipankara 64
Dolma Ling 89
*dorje see* vajra
Dorje Drakden 111
Dorje Lekpa 81
Drak Yerpa 56
Drepung *10*, 93, *93*
Drokmi 44
dualism 15
*duhkha* (suffering) 28, 29,
    30, *33*, 64, 116
Dur Bon 17
Dusum Chenpa 46, 51

ego, death of 37
Eight Auspicious Emblems
    105, *110–111*
Eightfold Path *see* Noble
    Eightfold Path 29
emptiness (*shunyata*) 32, 34,
    39, 40, 78, 121, 135
enlightenment *see* awakening
exorcism 109

festivals *10*, 94–99, *95*, *96*,
    *97*, *99*
First Diffusion of Buddhism
    32, 45
folk religion 12, 80–81

Foundation for the
    Preservation of the
    Mahayana Tradition 49
Four Noble Truths 29, 30
funerary rites 44, 122–125

Gampopa 45–46, 51, *55*
Ganden 46, *52*, 86
Ganden Tripa *52*
Garuda 77, *77*
*geko* (discipline monk)
    90–91, *95*
Gelukpa (school) 36, 46, 47,
    *52*, 61, *75*, 84, 86, 87,
    88, 93
Gendun Drup (Dalai Lama I)
    47, *47*, *52*
Gendun Gyatso (Dalai Lama
    II) *52*
Gesar Ling *16*, 17–18
ghosts 118
goddesses 70–73, 78–79
gods 74–77, 116
    Bon 80–81
"Great Fifth" Dalai Lama
    *52*, *52*, 85
Great Prayer Festival 46, 97
Gri Gum, King 17, *17*
Guru Rinpoche *see*
    Padmasambhava
*guru*s 48 *see also lamas*

hand *mandala 42*
Hayagriva *128*
heavens 119
hells 118, 119, *120*
Hevajra *48*, 98
*Hevajra Tantra* 44
Hilton, James 19
Himalayas 15
Hinayana 31, 64
Hinduism 34
*Homages to the Twenty-One
    Taras* 71, 73
horoscopes 106–107
human sacrifice 13

ignorance (*avidya*) 119–120,
    129
impermanence (*anitya*) 115,
    125
Iran 14, 15

*Jakata* stories 64
Jamyang Zhepa 90
Jokhang 20, 21, *21*, *34*
Jowo Rinpoche *20*, 21

Kadampa school 46–47
Kagyu *see* Kargyudpa
Kalachakra Mandala 41, *41*,
    *43*
Kargyudpa (Kagyupa) school
    36, 45–46, 54–55, 61, 79,
    98
*karma* 27, 107, 116, 117, 119
Karma Kargyud sect 51
Karmarpa Lama 46, 51, *51*,
    68
Khamtrul Rinpoche 89
Konchog Gyalpo 44
Kriyatantra 35, 36

Labrang Tashikyil 82, 90,
    96, 99, 120
*labrang*s 86
*lama*s 9, 27, 48–53, *48*, 86
    burial 125
    local healers 109–110
    teaching methods 76–77
    *see also* Dalai Lama
*Lamrim Chenmo* 46
Lang Darma, King 17, 22,
    23, 32, 44, 99
Langmusi 95
*Lankavatara Sutra* 31
*lha* (deities) 59
Lharampa 93
Lhasa 21, 86, 93, *102*, *104*
    Great Prayer Festival 46,
        97
    Jokhang 20, 21, *21*, *34*
    Potala 87, *87*

# PICTURE CREDITS

The publishers would like to thank the following individuals, museums and photographic libraries for permission to reproduce their material. Every care has been taken to trace copyright holders. However, if we have omitted anyone we apologize and will, if informed, make corrections in any future edition.

The list below includes descriptions of images and artworks that are uncaptioned in the main text of the book.

**Abbreviations:**

**DBP** Duncan Baird Publishers Archive
**TI** Tibet Images

**Page 1** Statue of Maitreya, the Buddha of the future, at Thikse monastery near Leh in Ladakh, India. TI; **2** Pilgrims burning offerings at dawn on Bompori Hill, Lhasa. TI/Ian Cumming; **6** Prayer flags leading to Tsemo monastery near Leh, Ladakh. Corbis/David Samuel Robbins; **10** Huge *thangka* on display at a festival, Drepung monastery. TI/Irene Slegt; **12** TI/Stone Routes; **13** Bon swastika. DBP/Private Collection; **14** Scenes from the story of the ogress Tagsen Mo and the monkey. DBP/Private Collection; **16** Spink's & Sons, London; **17** Gri Gum severs the cord linking him to heaven: *thangka* detail. DBP/Private Collection; **19** The kingdom of Shambala, 19th-century Mongolian *thangka* detail. John Bigelow Taylor, New York City/Musée Guimet, Paris; **20** TI/Ian Cumming; **21** Pilgrims in front of the Jokhang temple, Lhasa. TI/Catherine Platt; **22** Demon face

from Black Hat dancer's costume (commissioned artwork); **23** TI/B. Luther; **24** View over Samye monastery, Tibet. TI/Ian Cumming; **26** Prayer wheels at the Jokhang temple, Lhasa. TI/Ian Cumming; **28** TI/Ian Cumming; **29** Scenes from the life of the Buddha: Prince Siddhartha encounters death. Tibetan, 18th century. Art Archive/Musée Guimet, Paris/Dagli Orti; **30** British Museum (OA1973.5–14.1); **32** Detail of an old prayer book in Matho monastery, Ladakh. TI/Ian Cumming; **33** *Thankga*, late 17th century. John Bigelow Taylor, New York City/Private Collection of Robert Hatfield Ellsworth; **34** TI/Ian Cumming; **35** Bell and *vajra* on a prayer book table, Likir monastery, Ladakh. TI/Ian Cumming; **36** Gilt bronze *yab yum* statuette. Tibetan, 16th century. Bridgeman Art Library/Private Collection; **38** Prayer hall with a gilt statue of Padmasambhava, Hemis monastery, Ladakh. TI/Ian Cumming; **41** Kalachakra Mandala from central Tibet. Late 16th century. John Bigelow Taylor, New York City/ Musée Guimet, Paris; **42** Hands of a monk in *mandala mudra*. TI/Ian Cumming; **43** Central detail from the Kalachara Mandala shown on page 42. John Bigelow Taylor, New York City/Musée Guimet, Paris; **45** Detail of Padmasambhava from a *thangka*. Tibetan, 19th century. Art Archive/Private Collection, Paris/Dagli Orti; **46** Gilt bronze statuette of Tsong Khapa. Tibetan, 14th or 15th century. Art Archive/Musée Guimet, Paris/Dagli Orti; **47** TI/Ian

Cumming; **48** British Museum (OA1944,4–1.05); **49** Lama Tenzin Ösel Rinpoche, aged two. TI/Robin Bath; **51** H.H. Karmarpa XVII presenting a blessed cloth to a follower. Corbis/Sygma; **52** Art Archive/Musée Guimet, Paris/Dagli Orti; **53** H.H. Dalai Lama XIV at Dharamsala, 1990. TI/C.L.; **55** *Thangka* from eastern Tibet, 18th or 19th century. John Bigelow Taylor, New York City/Etnografiska Museet (National Museum of Ethnography), Stockholm; **56** View from Drak Yerpa, near Lhasa. TI/Mike Ford; **58** Prayer flags at a sacred spring in western Tibet. TI/Michael Shaw Bond; **60** Spink's & Sons, London; **61** The Adibuddha Vajrasattva seated on a lotus throne. Werner Forman Archive, London; **63** The Buddha Amitabha, Guarsai monastery, Amdo, Tibet. TI/Mike Ford; **65** The eleven heads of Avalokiteshvara, a bronze sculpture with turquoise inlay. Tibetan, 18th century. Art Archive/Musée Guimet, Paris/Dagli Orti; **66** Gilt bronze sculpture of Manjushri, *bodhisattva* of wisdom. Art Archive/Musée Guimet, Paris/Dagli Orti; **67** TI/Diane Barker; **69** TI/Ian Cumming; **70** John Bigelow Taylor, New York City/Royal Ontario Museum, Canada; **71** *mandala* of Green Tara. TI/Mike Ford; **72** Green Tara and the Assembly of the Twenty-One Taras. *Thangka* by Andy Weber, 1980; **75** *Thangka* of Yamantaka *yab yum*. Central Tibetan, late 17th or early 18th century. John Bigelow Taylor, New York City/The Zimmerman Family Collection; **76** TI/Mike Ford; **77** Garuda devouring a snake (commissioned artwork) 78 Dakini drinking demon blood from human skull cup. Late 17th-century *thangka*. Art Archive/Private Collection, Paris/Dagli Orti; 79 Statuette of Vajravarahi. John Bigelow Taylor, New York City/The Newark Museum; 81 British Museum (OA1980.3–26.1); 82 Prayer wheels at Labrang Tashikyil monastery, Amdo, eastern Tibet. TI/Ian Cumming; 84 TI/Ian Cumming; 85 *Chorten*s at Kumbum (Ta'er Si) monastery. TI/Ian Cumming; 87 The Potala, Lhasa. TI/Robin Bath; 88 Ordination ceremony for a young Tibetan monk. TI/Tenzin Dorje; 89 TI/Sean Sprague; 90 TI/Ian Cumming; 91 A young nun reading at Dolma Ling nunnery, Dharamsala. TI/Diane Barker; 92 Graham Harrison; 93 View of Drepung monastery. Corbis/Brian Vikander; 95 TI/Ian Cumming; 96 TI/Ian Cumming; 97 *Geko* (discipline monk) and assembly of monks, Nechung monastery. TI/Ian Cumming; 98 Detail of the Hevajra *mandala*. British Museum (OA1944,4–1.05); 99 Cham dancer at Labrang Tashikyil

monastery. TI/Ian Cumming; 100 TI/Mani Lama; 101 *Mani* stone at Dharamsala inscribed with *Om mani padme hum,* the *mantra* of Avalokiteshvara. TI/Ian Cumming; 102 Monks playing *dungchen* or long trumpets, Nechung monastery. TI/Ian Cumming; 103 Windhorse bearing wishfulfilling jewel (commissioned artwork); 104 TI/Ian Cumming; 106 TI/Sean Sprague; 107 Woman's amuletic necklace of amber, reputed to possess healing power. John Bigelow Taylor, New York City; 108 *Phurbu* ritual dagger. John Bigelow Taylor, New York City; 109 TI/Diane Barker; 111 Nechung oracle in a trance, May 1997. TI/Diane Barker; 112 *Thangka* of Vaishravana, guardian deity of the north and god of wealth. Central Tibet, early 15th century. John Bigelow Taylor, New York City/Private Collection of Robert Hatfield Ellsworth; 113 detail of the image on page 112; 114 Lama dance at Katok monastery festival. Corbis/Tiziana and Gianni Baldizzone; 117 wall painting of the Wheel of Life in Dip Tsechokling

monastery, Dharamsala. TI/Ian Cumming; 118 Depiction of Yama, bronze statue.Werner Forman Archive/British Library; 119 Heavenly wish-fulfilling tree, with its roots in the realm of the Jealous Gods and its fruits in the realm of the Gods (commissioned artwork); 120 TI/Ian Cumming; 122 Menia Hongyrang, Amdo. TI/Hamish Horsley; 123 *Chitipati*s (commissioned artwork); 124 Corbis/Brian A. Vikander; 125 Monks create a *mandala* of coloured sand at Simtokha, Bhutan. Corbis/Jeremy Horner; 126 monk reads prayers and collects alms on the Barkhor path. Corbis/Craig Lovell; 127 John Bigelow Taylor, New York City/The Newark Museum; 128 bronze statue, western Tibet, late 12th–early 13th century. John Bigelow Taylor, New York City/The Zimmerman Family Collection; 129 TI/Ian Cumming; 130–131 British Museum, London; 132 Bardo *mandala*. RMN, Paris; 133 Andy Weber, UK; 134 *ngakpa* (itinerant *yogin*) reciting from the *Bardo Thodol*. Corbis/Bennet Dean, Eye Ubiquitous